MY YEAR WITH THE WOODPECKERS

MY YEAR WITH
THE WOODPECKERS

HEINZ SIELMANN

TRANSLATED FROM THE GERMAN
BY SIDNEY LIGHTMAN

FOREWORD BY
JAMES FISHER

LONDON
BARRIE AND ROCKLIFF

MY SPECIAL THANKS ARE DUE TO
THE INSTITUTE FOR FILMS AND PICTURES
IN SCIENCE AND EDUCATION, MUNICH,
AND IN PARTICULAR TO THE DIRECTOR,
FRIDOLIN SCHMID, WHO COMMISSIONED
MY WORK WITH THE WOODPECKERS
AND MADE THIS BOOK POSSIBLE

PLATES

CONTENTS

FOREWORD

My friend Peter Scott's television programme 'Look', produced by the British Broadcasting Corporation's Natural History Unit from Bristol, has, over the course of a few years, quietly and inexorably become one of the most popular and compelling series of television broadcasts on any network of the United Kingdom. Its millions of faithful viewers look forward to the next number with constant loyalty and have seldom, if ever, been dissapointed. Yet 'Look' employs few of the tricks of presentation so beloved of the communications industry. It does not artificially create sensational situations; for the ordinary affairs of nature are sensational enough. None of the distinguished naturalists and cinematographers whom Peter Scott has introduced talk down to their public. Indeed, they talk, not to their public, so much as to each other in the relaxed yet lucid voices that they would use in any normal discussion of their profession amongst themselves. The fact that by so doing they capture and please their audience is itself proof that natural history needs no aids to acceptance and that the serious study of animals and plants has a mighty following.

Some people say that the popularity of natural history books, television and sound radio programmes derives from the wish of many of our industrialised population to escape; some even call this an escape from reality. If it is an escape it is an escape *to* reality, and one of the best signs that the human race is capable of conquering grave problems and of making our overcrowded world fit to live in.

In the forefront of the leadership of this new appreciation of nature are people like Heinz Sielmann and his colleagues at the *Institut fur Film and Bild* in Munich. They make nature films which are exciting, ingenious, accurate, philosophically honest and humane. They make them entirely without facetiousness or the tiresome tricks of those who seem driven all the time to compare animal behaviours with that of humans in a comic way.

I started this preface with a reference to the B.B.C.'s 'Look' programme because, in a sense, it was Heinz Sielmann who did much to put 'Look' on the map, and 'Look' which first introduced this remarkable naturalist to the British public. Needless to say, it was the subject of this book, Sielmann's woodpecker film, that created such a sensation on British television. The B.B.C. has a careful research group which accurately measures what they call the ' appreciation index ' of their television programmes. The A.I. for the woodpecker film on 'Look' was in the eighties—of the same order as that of the Cup Final and not far behind the Coronation! It was written about by all the critics, not all of whom (for reasons best known to themselves) normally discuss the nature features on television. It was repeated several times on the B.B.C.

The original film was specially edited for the 'Look' programme; and Heinz Sielmann personally appeared in the studio with Peter Scott. He has done so several times since with other beautiful, equally successful, films. After this success the original woodpecker film, made for the Institute's educational distribution on the Continent, was distributed in Britain by the Educational Foundation for Visual Aids, and the writer of this preface had the pleasure of adapting and speaking the English commentary. Through the English school and nature societies it must, by now, have been seen by tens of thousands of people, young and old.

I am sure the reasons for Heinz Sielmann's success are very simple ones. First of all comes his scientific integrity. He has a first-rate scholar's knowledge of the animals he works with. Before embarking on the beautiful programme of work with the woodpeckers described in this book he thoroughly familiarised himself with the species and with what had been already learned and published about them in scientific journals. His campaign was designed as a true expedition with almost military precision, and he allowed no other activities, or any considerations of time, to interfere with his work or the work of his able colleagues. Above all, his year with the woodpeckers was spent with ingenuity. Nobody before Sielmann had ever thought of the possibility of filming wild woodpeckers, and black woodpeckers at that, *in the nest*. The fact that he was able to do so with a minimum of disturbance to the woodpeckers is a tribute to his skill, humanity and patience.

I greet this book as a monument to the dedicated labour that goes into the making of a first-rate nature film today. But it is not only the story of a successful campaign. It is the story of a group of extremely beautiful birds, the woodpeckers of Europe, from which the bird-watcher and the scientific naturalist can learn much. What I am trying to say is that it is a contribution to ornithological research, as well as to education. And Sielmann has written his account of it in much the way as he made his famous film: with felicity, economy, lack of sentimentality. He has let the fascinating facts speak for themselves, and he has been well served by his translator. Since *Woodpeckers*, Heinz Sielmann has made several other interesting original and beautiful films, and let us hope he writes books about them. If they are as good as this one they will be very good indeed.

July 1959   JAMES FISHER

ONE

On the Track of the Woodpeckers

I told the forester what I wanted to do.

'I have no objection at all,' said old Hummel, 'if you content yourself with filming the woodpeckers outside their nests as they run up tree trunks, and bore nesting holes and feed their young. But (he went on) this scheme of yours, to record all their activities inside their nests—not to mention filming them at their anvils, and searching for food in tree trunks and anthills—Why, it's absurd. You'd better give up the whole idea. Nothing will come of it, anyway.'

I had brought along shots from my earlier films which added up to quite a lot of hard work with animals, but Hummel would not be convinced. 'You may know the forest very well and have made a lot of complicated animal films,' he said, 'but your woodpecker programme will never work out. You'd better give up the whole idea.'

I had made the acquaintance of Hummel two years earlier when filming for the Max Planck Institute in neighbouring Buldern. In its silence and solitude the stretch of forest which he had tended for fifty years was an ideal haunt for woodpeckers. Now I had the opportunity of making a complete film about them; and it was quite clear to me that I would never find a more suitable spot.

All I had to do now was convince the forester that my plan for the woodpeckers was at least worth a try—and above all to get his agreement to the shooting of the film.

It took a long discussion to get Hummel interested at all in my working methods, but finally he said: 'All right, I'll let you make films in my forest, and will also help you as far as I can, but don't blame me later on when you find you have been to a lot of trouble for nothing.'

So I got the old forester's agreement, but of course I had to make clear to him what effects my activities might have on this quiet stretch of forest land—involving as they did cameras with telescopic lenses, sound equipment and all the paraphernalia connected with them. I also had to point out to him that we would have to fell a great number of pine trees in order to build our hides, and that we planned to cut away parts of some trees to get at the nesting holes. This would render them worthless from the forestry point of view.

The forester listened reflectively to my description of what I intended to do. I was afraid he would retort that he could not be expected to condone wanton damage of that kind. Instead, he said in quite a friendly manner: 'If you really want to go to so much trouble for these wood-peckers the forest will also play its part. There is fir copse where the trees stand so thickly that it will be good for them if a few are chopped down. And as far as opening up the nest holes is concerned, we'll deal with each case on its merits. Some of the woodpeckers live in old trees anyway, and they are only worth using for firewood. Even if the nest holes which are suitable for you are in good timber, I will still be able to help you with a clear conscience.'

After supper I made a few more sketches to illustrate how we planned to make our hides and open up the woodpeckers' nesting-holes. Forester Hummel had a wide experience of building hides, and studied my sketches with professional interest. 'In theory that's well thought out,' said, 'but how it will work in practice depends on the woodpeckers.'

The forester was seventy-two, so nine o'clock was bedtime for him, but before we said our goodnights he cautioned me again. 'You have, taken on a tough proposition, and you want to get a decent return for all the time and money you are going to invest. You'd better think the whole thing over. In my opinion your plan has very little chance of success.'

I had taken up quarters in the attic of his house in order to perfect my plans and make all the most important preparations for my year with the woodpeckers. In front of the open window the golden moonlight shone over the treetops through a veil of rain. The first scents of spring drifted into the room and the cry of a tawny owl mingled with the drumming of a snipe making its courting flight over the clearing.

It was the proper setting in which to reconsider quietly the pros and cons of our project. Hummel's verdict of 'impossible' was not completely unjustified. Many prominent zoologists had expressed the same opinion in answer to my questions. Moreover, I knew that the life of the woodpeckers in their nesting holes, and the movements of their tongues, had never been recorded by any observer—many activities of importance for our films took place under cover of the shadowy tree tops. However, anyone whose chosen profession is the observation and filming of animals must have the courage to broaden his activities and experiments with the woodpeckers would no doubt provide the most fascinating problems.

Since my childhood, when I made closer acquaintance with the black woodpecker during my schooldays in East Prussia, woodpeckers had been my special love. It had undoubtedly been love at first sight; as I sat over my sketches that evening in the forest I saw in my mind's eye a very clear picture of that magical eastern landscape with its forests and lakes, its steep shores, its moving sand dunes and its marshes—everything that year by year, had driven me while still a schoolboy into nature observation.

Hardly one of those days went by—especially in the spring—without my making a foray over the coastal fields or into the surrounding forests. It was there that I laid all sorts of ambushes under cover of which my dream of a cloak of invisibility came true. In well-camouflaged hides it is possible to remain concealed from even the shyest creatures, and so

15

strongly did the thrill of unimpeded closeness to wild animals take hold of me, that eventually my parents and teachers acquiesced in my apparently aimless wanderings, though with misgivings. My wanderings did not remain aimless as I strove to gain an insight into the life and habits of individual animals through planned observations. My first choice fell on the marsh waders in the meadows near the bay. Courtships, nesting habits, the management of broods by parents—the study of all these things wonderfully repaid all my efforts, since nothing much was then known of the life of those birds.

To document my observations for the experts I became a proficient photographer, particularly with telescopic lenses. In a short time I had made so many promising observations that, although only a fifth-former, I was invited to report on my work as a naturalist to a scientific gathering. The cordial reception which greeted my début silenced all opposition at home to my passionate interest in nature study. At school, too, my teachers now and then turned a blind eye to my comings and goings when I was compelled, at all costs, to get to nests where I knew that some special event was about to take place.

During the Easter holidays in the following year I had planned to observe the breeding habits of the heron in the Masurian forests, and it was then that I had my first unforgettable encounter with the black woodpecker.

Masuria was so rich in old stands of timber that in many parts of the forest nature could be left to her own devices. Ageing trees were allowed to stand until storms brought them down. In countless pinewoods the golden eagle still reigned supreme, and nobody grudged the swooping ospreys the fish they snatched from the lakes when foraging for their young. The active yet stealthy flight of the black storks above the towering tree tops was a daily sight: and among some hundred-and-fifty-year-old pines the big herons had built up a colony of a hundred nests or more. Their nests were in the spreading branches up eighty feet or so, and if I wanted to see what went on in the nests I had to build a hide at least

At the beginning of March we moved into woodpecker territory

When the snow melts the great tit's thaw song rings through the forest . . .

. . . and the woodpeckers can be heard loudly drumming away

The black woodpecker had chosen a branch at the top of a tree for his xylophone . . .

. . . while the great spotted woodpecker preferred a side-branch, which gave his drumming much more resonance

three feet higher than this. This was not easy, but I managed it in two days and the following morning—at the end of March—I climbed up there before daybreak to spend the whole spring day in the tree tops as an invisible guest of the herons. The East Prussian winter, which is often severe, had not yet loosened its grip on the forests. There were deep snowdrifts under fir trees and juniper bushes, for changing weather, with snow and hail showers, had delayed the thaw. After the night's rain the forest flamed into life at daybreak with sparkling rain drops everywhere, and echoed with the early spring songs of the birds.

Soon, while the sun was still low, blue-grey ramparts of cloud began towering up into the sky. The bright morning suddenly became dark, the song-birds grew silent, the branches creaked and bent under the force of the storm, and then the hail started. It came down so thickly and fiercely that I could hardly see the ground at all from my hide. The storm lasted only a few minutes; and then broad shafts of sunlight were streaming through the branches and tree trunks again, shining on the steaming earth. The great herons, standing quite unmoved on their nests, shook beads of water from their plumage and settled down on their nests again. As if by some pre-arranged signal the dawn chorus broke forth again in the frosty, crystal-clear air—the dreamy melody of the robin, the trills of the blue tit, the solemn measures of the song thrush, and the mewing of the buzzard—falling in great swoops from the deep blue sky almost to the tree tops in his courtship flight.

Suddenly a call rang out that I had never heard before. The clear, steady 'krrri-krrri-krrri-' was so impressive that I tried at once to spot the strange bird. The thick foliage at the back of the hide blocked my view; but then I heard, quite close, a heavy beating of wings and in a moment a noise like the slap of a half-open hand on a tree trunk. A black wood-pecker had alighted hardly two yards from me. He was the size of a crow, and for a few moments remained in the typical woodpecker stance on the trunk of a tree. This was long enough for me to print his appearance firmly on my memory.

17

B

The upper part of his body was steeply inclined backwards, his weight resting on his tail of hard, tapering feathers with powerful, flexible quills. His big bluish-grey feet had two half-moon-shaped claws in front, one at the back, and one turned towards the side like a sort of rudder; these gave him a sure grip, even on a smooth tree trunk. The soft black of his plumage was unrelieved by any other colour, even in that hard light, which was why the fiery red of his crown stood out so effectively. This combination of colour brought out particularly the sulphur-yellow of his eyes and the ivory colour of his powerful beak.

The crimson crown identified the bird as a male; and he was obviously seeking a mate, because at intervals he would send his call of 'kleea' ringing through the forest, looking to right and left with neck outstretched, and swinging from side to side on the tree trunk. Finally he ran nimbly up the tree to a withered branch. At each step he sprang swiftly upwards, with his head jerking outwards in staccato movement. At the same time his pointed claws gripped the bark unerringly, like climbing irons, while his weight was supported from below by his tail. When my woodpecker had almost reached the end of the branch, I realised that he was making for a specific place that he already knew about. With short, light hops, he reached a safe position, threw back his head and began drumming on the 'xylophone' he had chosen for himself. So fast was his drumming that it was impossible, even at that short distance, to see the movements of his beak. The woodpecker repeated his drumming performance five times before hurrying off with a jay-like flight. I heard the sound of his wings for a little while until the trees swallowed him up.

The significance of this drumming was at that time lost on me, though it obviously had nothing to do with boring a nesting hole or searching for food. Nor could I understand how the bird's skull could stand up to its powerful drumming on dry wood. My interest in woodpeckers had been aroused and from then on I became keener and keener to track down these strange birds of the forest and record their remarkable activities on film. But the more I thought about it the clearer the difficulties became. The many operations carried out with the beak—drumming, hollowing out a nesting hole, searching for food, and others—mostly took place high up in the trees, concealed by branches or foliage. How would it be possible to observe these birds closely? After all, they were not obliged to live close to a place where there was room for a hide big enough to take men and equipment! It seemed to me, then, quite impossible to find an 'open sesame' to the woodpeckers. Without observations and photographs of their activities inside their dwellings, the year with the woodpeckers I dreamed of must remain just wishful thinking.

Later on, during a spell of nearly ten years of biological and film work for the Institute for Films and Pictures in Science and Education, I had plenty of time to plan a film about woodpeckers. Very often, when productions were mooted, new working methods had to be developed. Squirrels rearing their young enclosed in a nest of twigs; the life of the hamster in its underground system of burrows; the activities of bumble bees in their hive in an abandoned mole's burrow; the way frogs and toads croak (which can usually only be filmed in darkness): these were some of my assignments. On the strength of some success with these I felt I could at last dare to try and make a film of the life of the wood-peckers inside their tree trunk nesting holes.

Of all the animals, including birds that I have worked with, the woodpeckers are my favourites; and this is not only because my film of them achieved an unusual measure of success, but also because I was able to find out many new facts about the biology of these birds. This is why this book gives not only an account of *my* experiences in making the film, but a detailed description of the most important happenings in the woodpeckers' lives.

TWO

Our European Woodpeckers

Woodpeckers are cosmopolitan and inhabit every part of the world except Madagascar and the Australian region, but their haunts are not restricted to forests. In the American desert they hollow out nesting holes in the stems of the tallest cactuses; in the African plain I have found their nesting places in the trunks of *Euphorbia candelabrum* trees.

The woodpeckers most commonly found in Europe prefer to nest in mixed forests where deciduous trees outnumber the conifers, though great spotted woodpeckers and lesser spotted woodpeckers spread out to copses, gardens and orchards. Here the lesser spotted woodpecker, the smallest of his species, becomes a real acrobat, foraging for fruit pests right to the very tip of every branch. Green woodpeckers and grey-headed woodpeckers are particularly well-established in more open woodland; only the black woodpecker—as big as a crow, and the shyest of them all—prefers larger, quieter forests.

Woodpeckers are non-migratory birds and, if food supply allows, will stay in the same part of the forest throughout the year. The black woodpecker will forage for food for distances up to several miles from its hole, even at nesting time, and in winter will range even further afield to find its main diet of ants. When food is scarce the great spotted woodpecker lives on fir and pine cone seeds, often scouring a wide area for them.

In February, when the thaw sets in, bringing the first promise of spring—sometimes even in January—the woodpeckers gather, and their haunts resound to their drumming. The forest where I spent my year with the woodpeckers is not far from Dülmen in Westphalia, in an area drained by the Rhine, the Ruhr, the Lippe and the Ems. It is a mixed forest covering no more than twelve hundred and fifty acres of beeches, oaks, larches and pines, surrounded by young plantations gradually giving way to pasture and arable land. This small, privately-owned forest had taken my fancy at the time of my first visit. I found many old trees there, especially tall beeches which had long ago reached an age when they were ready for axe and saw to reduce them to logs. But the owner loved his forest and hardly exploited it commercially, so the woodpeckers could live there quite undisturbed. The forest was full of wild life which promised well for observation and film work. My co-worker, George Schimanski, and I counted three pairs of black woodpeckers, two pairs of green woodpeckers and six pairs of great spotted woodpeckers in a comparatively restricted area. This meant that we had three totally different members of the woodpecker family whose life and habits we could compare. So the choice was made and the decision taken. A year with the woodpeckers lay before us, still a closed book like the other secrets of the small forest which was to be our home for many months.

THREE

The Drumming in the Tree Tops

Two weeks after my conversation with Hummel, George Schimanski and I had set up our headquarters in the woodpecker forest. It was the middle of March; but spring was late that year. There had been snow showers and night frost earlier in the month, so the drumming of wood-peckers, on which we had hoped to concentrate, was not fully under way. Instead we spent the changeable, early spring days discovering their various haunts and noting the favourite drumming trees.

All woodpeckers have numerous drumming trees in their nesting area and visit them all at irregular intervals.

We had to get as close as possible to the birds to film their beak movements during this strange activity, and so we had to find a drumming tree in a spot where we could build a hide. Several days passed before we could decide on the right place, because the stormy weather kept the woodpeckers away; moreover the abundance of drumming trees always found at the beginning of the year made our choice extremely difficult.

To give resonance and carrying power to the roll of their beaks, woodpeckers prefer to drum on dry branches, as near the top of the tree as possible, usually thirty to fifty feet from the ground. We were delighted, therefore, to discover a much-visited site in the top of a wild cherry tree only twenty-five feet from the ground. The distance from the branch to the centre of the tree top—where a hide could be built—was nine feet, just right for close-ups of drumming woodpeckers. Any disturbance during drumming would only cause the bird to fly away somewhere else; so we chose the afternoon of a rainy, windy day for building our hide. It was unlikely that any woodpecker would visit his drumming tree in such weather. We started building the hide, as we had often done when photographing birds of prey, by nailing a square of four-inch pine stakes to the limbs of the tree. On these we laid boards to form a platform on which we erected our film equipment. The hide was then thickly walled round with pine branches and twigs, so that no hint of our occupancy would attract the attention of even the sharpest-eyed woodpecker.

The weather changed on March 20th and a warm west wind blew through the forest; even at night the temperature remained some degrees above freezing. At last we were able to make a start with recording the drumming of the great spotted woodpeckers.

We were already in position in the woodpecker area before sunrise, waiting for the drumming to begin. As the stars paled in the sky, the thrushes, mere silhouettes on the pine trees, began their songs. Then, far below us in the bushes, the call of the robin was heard, shy and tender as if in a dream. The wood-pigeons joined in with their low-keyed cooing. There is truly no more delightful experience than to listen to the forest waking to the dawn. Soon the wren added its trills to the morning chorus, so loud and sustained that they seemed to come from a much larger bird.

Daylight came with the singing of the finches; and at the same time the drumming of a woodpecker could be heard in the distance, taking its part in the many-voiced concert of the birds. The drummers of the bird world wake comparatively late, which is quite understandable since they sleep in holes in the trunks of trees (except in the incubating period) and are only roused by the growing light outside. Soon woodpeckers could be heard all round us. At that time I had not yet learned to distinguish the drumming of the various species of woodpecker. We had first to discover how closely the great spotted woodpecker's drumming resembled that of the black woodpecker and the points of difference which would

23

enable us to tell them apart. However, we hoped that our observations would make this increasingly easy.

We did not have to wait long for our great spotted woodpecker. With a loud 'kik' he landed quite close to us on his drumming branch. He spent some time inspecting our hide thoroughly and we could see that he felt that there was something rather unusual going on. Nevertheless, after a little while, down flashed his beak and he started drumming, paying no further attention to our hide. Meanwhile, we filmed his technique from three yards away, using a powerful lens with a focal length of 600 millimetres. But we met with unexpected difficulties. In the first place, we could not keep the camera turning as fast as the bird was drumming. A woodpecker always begins its drumming by raising its head high and then bringing it down sharply. Every now and again it breaks off and jerks its head briskly from side to side, inspecting the results of its diligence. These spontaneous movements made it extremely difficult to time the moment when the next burst of drumming would begin. In addition, it appeared that we had not muffled the camera sufficiently for the close range at which we were working, and its whirring irritated our woodpecker. The unseen competition proved too much for him and put him off completely. Only when we had placed a soundproof cover over the camera were we successful in getting our first pictures of him drumming.

We had made it a rule to send off every day's work the same evening so that we could know with the least possible delay whether the films were adequate for our purpose. This precaution is essential in nature photography, since many important things in the life cycle of animals take place only on certain days of the year. If the observer should learn too late that certain shots vital to his film have not been successful, he may have to wait a whole year before he gets an opportunity to re-shoot them. There are further difficulties, too. Not only can valuable time be lost, but it is almost impossible for conditions to be exactly similar a year later when films have to be re-shot in the same spot.

It was a good job that we took precautions with our shots of wood-peckers drumming. We had exposed the first few reels at the normal rate of twenty-four frames a second, but the woodpecker's beak shuttled up and down so swiftly that the camera barely registered four of the average of eight strokes in each burst of drumming. When these films were pro-jected they gave the impression that the woodpecker was striking the branch with his beak in search of food, not drumming against it fast and furiously. It was easy to correct this false impression by increasing the rate of exposure to forty frames a second and extending the time, so that the film recorded every phase of the beak movements during drumming.

Before the male black woodpecker finds a mate he will drum some five or six hundred times a day, as Pynnönen has established. When a bird was extraordinarily excited the rate of drumming rose to ten bursts a minute, each at the rate of six to ten strokes every half second. That the woodpecker's beak, and not only his beak but his brain can withstand such a hammering both when he is drumming and when he is tunnelling his nesting hole—is due to the special anatomy of his skull. The bones between beak and cranium are not rigidly joined as they are in other birds. The connective tissue is spongy and elastic. A complicated mechanism ensures that every time a blow is struck with the beak the shock is broken by the flexible cartilage connecting the root of the beak to the bones of the skull.

But to return to the woodpecker's drumming and its purpose. Laymen almost always think, when they hear this loud drumming, that the woodpecker—the carpenter of the forest—is either making a hole in a tree trunk or searching for food. In fact, the loud hammer blows of the woodpecker's beak are signals, almost a kind of instrumental music, whereby he can communicate with other woodpeckers up to three quarters of a mile away. Just as song-birds with their varied trills and calls entice females of the same species to come and nest in their territory, and warn rival males of ownership, so the woodpecker has his own special call—his drumming—which can be heard for much greater distances than any

25

bird song. This drumming is the most significant of the woodpecker's activities, for it is an invitation to a female of the species to join him in boring a nesting hole, and a declaration to rival males that he owns the territory around it.

The multiplicity of drumming places may seem to contradict this, since not only we, but the woodpeckers also were uncertain as to exactly which bird was drumming. The apparent contradiction is explained by the fact that until pairing is completed, male and hen birds are continually on the move in their habitat, exploring different places. Once courting has begun, however, they restrict themselves to one main drumming branch. We were thus able, in the course of our observations, to distinguish the various 'personalities' among the woodpeckers.

Having spent more than a week observing the drumming of the great spotted woodpecker we decided to investigate the black woodpeckers. We had already kept a look-out for their favourite drumming places, but they visited them much less frequently than the great spotted woodpeckers and the sound almost always came from a different spot. When the pair-bond has been cemented and the birds have begun to bore their nesting hole, the spate of drumming tails off, and we wanted to make the most of every opportunity; we accordingly set up our camera every morning in one of the spots which our earlier observations had shown us the black woodpeckers visited at least once a day. Despite this, several weeks went by without our being able to get even one picture.

We were quite used to long waits in our work with animals; and we accepted delays patiently as long as they did not jeopardise other important film work. In this case, however, it soon became clear that we had been fighting a losing battle, for the black woodpeckers had already paired off and no longer needed to attract a mate with their drumming.

Meanwhile, April was drawing to a close. The beech buds burst into leaf and the first veils of fresh green began to shroud the bare branches. Soon it would be almost impossible to film the woodpeckers in the shade of the tree-tops. We decided to resort to a trick. We had

26

already noticed that our woodpeckers began drumming busily whenever a strange woodpecker, not yet paired off, appeared in the forest searching for a mate. The black woodpecker male would immediately begin drumming at a tremendous rate in order to show his anger at seeing an intruder. We had also noticed that, after nest hole boring had begun in late spring the great spotted woodpeckers were quick to start drumming as soon as there was any disturbance near their nesting sites. The drumming of the woodpeckers can be seen, therefore, to have two purposes. At pairing time it indicates where they are going to hollow out their nesting holes; when a rival appears it means: 'Keep out! This is my home!'

It looked as if we ourselves would have to be the intruders, and lure the woodpeckers to a specific place. And then we had a stroke of luck! As George was preparing to play back the spotted woodpecker sound recordings, a black woodpecker flew up, took possession of its smaller relative's drumming branch and began to hammer away at it. There were only a few strokes, but we recorded them because they could be extraordinarily useful to us.

Next morning we set up a loudspeaker near the black woodpeckers' tree and ran a lead from it to our tape recorder a hundred yards away. Then we played back the drumming we had recorded the day before, over and over again at frequent intervals. By varying the volume we created the impression of a strange woodpecker ranging through the area, drumming wherever he alighted. We continued like this for half an hour without result. The hen bird was in the hole in the tree, and looked out several times as if astonished, but apart from this seemed quite unperturbed by the strange concert. Then came the time for the change-over. We had heard the male calling from some distance away, and now he arrived at his tree. He had hardly alighted when we greeted him with a staccato burst of drumming. It was overwhelmingly successful. Boring the nesting hole and taking over guard duty were alike forgotten as the black woodpecker leapt to his drumming. So anxious was he to start that he did not bother with his tried and trusted drumming place. Instead, in his excitement, he belaboured a totally unsuitable branch which did not have the correct resonance.

He searched for the ghostly peace-breaker for almost half an hour. We could certainly have kept him at it for much longer, but we could not manage to stalk him with the camera. As soon as we painstakingly got to within fifty yards of him he changed his position. Just the same, we were very satisfied with the result of our experiment. We had found our woodpecker's favourite drumming place, and now prepared a suitable hide for some filming.

We left the woodpecker in peace for a day, but the morning after that, under a cloudless sky, we set up our film equipment in the hide and sent our sound recordings ringing through the forest. As before, the hen bird was indifferent to the sound of our drumming, while the male searched even more fiercely for his invisible rival. We were able several times to lure him within a few yards of our hide and film him in close-up.

The sound recording we used played for four minutes, beginning with the great spotted woodpecker's drumming and ending with the black woodpecker's staccato hammer blows. When we played the recording in areas inhabited by both species, it was always the great spotted woodpecker which answered first. The black woodpecker responded only when he heard the drumming of his rival of the same species. This indicated that each woodpecker recognises the drumming rhythm of its own particular species. Later on, when we had accumulated a great deal of recorded material, we played back the drumming so slowly that we were able to count the strokes. From this analysis we established that great spotted woodpeckers strike their 'xylophones' twelve to fourteen times for each burst and that the duration of a burst of drumming is .76 to .98 seconds. The figures for the black woodpecker were thirty-five to forty-four blows with the beak and a duration of from 2.1 to 2.69 seconds. This means that the black woodpecker's drumming lasts about three times as long as that of the great spotted woodpecker, and, because of its heavier beak, is in a lower key. It was not difficult, therefore, for us to distinguish them even from a distance.

The drumming calls and replies of the woodpeckers we were studying were quite separate and alternated with each other, whereas the American red-bellied woodpeckers have developed community drumming. I would like to draw attention to this difference in the habits of the European and the American species. Lawrence Kilham has observed that the ceremony begins with the male standing at the entrance to his hole and calling the hen with a tuneful 'knirr-knirr'. As soon as the hen flies up to him, the male conceals himself inside the nesting hole and begins making his way towards the entrance, drumming as he goes. Meanwhile the hen is engaged in drumming from the outside, so that although they are separated from each other their drumming is synchronised. Eventually the male emerges and both birds stand shoulder to shoulder hammering away at the hole in unison. This behaviour demonstrates very clearly the significance of drumming in the search for a mate, in pairing, and in the decision to tunnel out a common nesting hole.

FOUR

Courtship and Nest Choosing

If a woodpecker should be in courting mood as early as February its drumming is in most cases a completely one-sided announcement of the fact. At this time a hen bird on a courting flight can even fly right up to a male without diverting him from his search for food. But as the days grow warmer, usually at the end of March, pairing and the selection of living quarters begin.

At pairing time the woodpecker areas are really noisy. Both males and hens drum busily away, not having adapted themselves to each other at this early stage. Intruding rivals are generally driven off by the male quickly because even woodpeckers feel handicapped outside their own territories; wildly noisy pursuit flights also take place among couples of the same species.

Woodpeckers are definite individualists and they learn only slowly to live together. To learn to recognise each other they employ a special ceremony. For example, if a male sees another woodpecker in his area he overtakes it in flight; they then both alight and stand facing each other for a little while, with their beaks outstretched. It could well be that up to this point they have not recognised each other as being male and hen bird—since their drumming is identical, they have the same calls and any differences in their plumage are slight.

At this first confrontation (usually with a tree trunk between them) they keep their beaks pointing towards each other and swing them back and forth continuously threatening one another—each bird using its swinging beak to keep the other at a distance. But suddenly, a turn of the head will reveal their distinguishing markings to each other. (With European woodpeckers, the distinguishing markings are on the head). Their threats then turn into a charming courtship.

These affairs were first observed in the flicker, an American woodpecker which is the counterpart of our green woodpecker. In this species the only difference between the plumage of the two sexes is the male's black moustachial stripe. In order to test his observations and conclusions, Noble painted these male markings on a hen woodpecker after pairing. The result was that she was taken for a rival male and driven off.

The progressive stages from first contact to final pairing have since been confirmed from the study of other species. The main distinguishing marking of the male green woodpecker is the red centre of its broad black moustachial stripe. He shows this to the hen bird in the same way as the flicker and with the same result. The black woodpecker's marking is red. It extends over the top of the male's head, while the hen just has a smallish red patch on the back of her head. When the two birds confront each other, they stretch their beaks outwards and upwards, swinging them in a series of elipses so that the red markings show up better than if they merely swung their beaks backwards and forwards.

When the courting ceremony is over the pair usually remain faithful to each other, and at the end of March they begin preparations for boring a hole. By ringing woodpeckers it has been possible to establish that in most cases it is the hen which chooses the nesting area. Loos was able to discover that the black woodpecker hen remains true to her chosen area while on the other hand the male changes his area in successive breeding seasons. Blume observed that in twenty pairs of green wood-peckers it was the hens' winter roosting holes which, almost without exception, were chosen as breeding places.

In the selection of a site for the hole itself it is the male's choice

31

which is decisive; and he is the more active partner throughout the whole nesting time. The birds can often be seen searching for a dwelling place together. The male flies up to suitable holes and offers them to the hen for inspection by repeatedly looking inside and then out again. In our Dülmen forest no black woodpecker or great spotted woodpecker pair had the good fortune to find a hole, because a truly imposing number of bird usurpers had already occupied them.

Every year the woodpeckers become carpenters again for a time, a business which, as we shall see, provides living quarters for quite a number of other species which nest in holes. The green woodpecker is in rather a special position; his beak is weaker and somewhat bent and therefore not so suitable for carpentry. He therefore prefers to move into a nesting hole left over from the previous year. Where this is not possible, the green woodpecker seeks out a rotten tree, soft and wormy to its very core.

At the start of their building activities the woodpeckers seem to be very selective, going from tree to tree making small holes with their beaks. But this is not, as might be supposed, to test the firmness of the wood, and find soft places which would offer less resistance to their beaks. There were many kinds of tree in our part of the forest and we could tell from our observations that any kind of tree trunk was considered suitable for making nesting holes. The black woodpecker, in fact, even seemed to have a preference for hard trees. He liked beechwood best of all; and in many cases made holes in perfectly sound beech trunks, as we could see from the chips of wood which littered the ground.

Some naturalists have suggested that the small holes made in the early spring are a preparation for future work and are designed to rot the openings in the trunk by exposing them to the weather. But this theory does not seem to be correct. A great number of observations have confirmed that the woodpecker finishes his carpentering work without interruption even on trees with perfectly sound trunks. These first steps in building are part of the ceremony of pairing. Just as some other birds

32

Our pair of great spotted
woodpeckers had hollowed
out their nesting
hole in twelve days

Woodpeckers do not need
to bring nesting material from
outside

The fine wood-chips left over
from hole-tunnelling operations
make a bed for the eggs

Two of the birds which exploit
woodpecker's excavations

The nuthatch usually takes over
the holes of the great spotted
woodpecker. To protect its home
against intruders it walls up
the entrance, leaving only
a small opening

The hoopoe needs more
living space and rears its young
in the holes
of the green woodpecker

Only the male great spotted
woodpecker has a red nape-patch.
The young of both sexes
have a red crown

The great spotted woodpeckers
flew up to their hole
with food forty-three times
in seven hours

When sixteen days old
the nestlings began climbing up
to the entrance of the hole
as soon as they heard
the parent birds arrive with food

make model nests at pairing time the woodpecker makes miniature holes. It may be assumed that by doing this, the pair are striving to cement their union until their nesting urge becomes so powerful that actual building can begin.

C

FIVE

Carpenters of the Forest

A new part of the yearly cycle had begun for the woodpeckers—the excavation of the nesting hole. We had intended to observe, and film from the very beginning, the carpentering activities of the woodpeckers— particularly the way they worked with their chisel-like beaks. But this was easier said than done. After only two days the work of these diligent carpenters would be so far advanced that their busily chiselling beaks would be barely visible outside the tree trunk. This led to many disappointments for us.

When we heard a woodpecker hammering we used the succeeding pause to begin constructing a hide. Woodpeckers usually cut at a height of fifteen to thirty-two feet from the ground, black woodpeckers often even higher. A hide suitable for our purposes could not be built quickly, for any woodpecker would certainly have taken it amiss had we suddenly erected a strange edifice hard by his building site. We needed at least two days for each job, and each time we started constructing a hide, the woodpecker would finish work before us, and start hammering again somewhere else. This constant change of building site at this stage had actually nothing to do with us. Our only chance lay in approaching carefully, building a concealed hide, and observing the woodpeckers when they finally did get down to tunnelling in earnest.

At the beginning of April their hammering resounded through the forest from morning till night. This made it easy to find their individual sites and set up a suitable hide. Our best one was at the building site of a great spotted woodpecker pair some thirteen feet up in a birch tree. Despite the heavy snowfalls of the previous winter, the tall, thickly-growing ferns had remained unbent, sheltered as they were by the trees, and it was easy to build a hide under cover of them, quite close to the woodpeckers.

Woodpeckers begin boring their holes by chiselling out wedges from selected places on the tree trunk. Their rhythm and technique are quite different from those used in drumming. During drumming a woodpecker bends his head back as a preliminary to furiously fast bursts of drumming, with his neck outstretched and his beak kept close to the tree trunk. But when tunnelling, the bird uses the swing of neck and head. Holding himself fast to the tree with his claws, and using his tail as a support, he bends the upper part of his body back slightly to put the greatest possible force behind every swing of his beak. Anything from three to fifteen blows of the beak are necessary to produce a wood chip a quarter of an inch to one and a quarter inches long.

The woodpecker extends and deepens the hole horizontally by hammering with head aslant, first from the right then from the left. As soon as he starts in earnest the great spotted woodpecker is impelled by a feverish urge to work. He will hammer away up to six hours a day, often for more than an hour at a time. After four or five bursts of hammering he throws out the chips which have accumulated in the hole with a sharp sideways motion of his head and then resumes his hammering with un-reduced vigour. Although we know how the woodpecker's head can withstand this tremendous strain, we must still admire the strength and energy of this small bird, no bigger than a starling. Not only are the head and neck muscles at full stretch during the continuous, heavy hammering, but great demands are also made on the bird's feet and tail—in fact on his whole body.

Immediately behind the woodpeckers' tree there was a path much frequented by hikers. As soon as anybody approached within twenty yards, the woodpecker would hop into cover behind the tree, where it was difficult to see him against the speckled black and white of the bark. It was as if he were deliberately playing hide and seek, ensuring in his progress round the tree that he always kept the trunk between him and any passer-by. By the time the coast was clear, he would have completed the circle, made sure that he was safe and would then resume his work.

Among great spotted woodpeckers the hen does less than half the work of nest building, sometimes even leaving it almost entirely to the male; and the pair we were observing were no exception. Most of the time the hen stayed close to the hole; and we heard her give warning whenever people passed by, or a sparrow-hawk swept through the forest on a hunting expedition. Several times a day the hen would offer herself to the male for mating. This soliciting actually begins before hole tunnelling starts, but from then on it is a daily event until the incubation period. When the woodpecker makes a nuptial flight his soaring progress bears no resemblance at all to his usual strong, undulating flight. His head is sunk between the shoulders, the tail raised a little and the wings spread slightly. His crimson under tail-coverts, the distinguishing markings of the great spotted woodpecker, can be seen from some way away. It should be mentioned that woodpeckers often make the same soaring flight when an intruding woodpecker appears near their holes during nesting time.

Whenever our hen woodpecker visited the building site she would look inside the (as yet unfinished) hole with great interest, as if to inspect her mate's work and see what progress he had made. Finally she would throw out the wood chippings still left inside and do a bit of hammering herself. Very shortly afterwards, she would unhurriedly clean her plumage, rest a while on the tree trunk and then fly off. Her personal contribution to making the hole was notably small, although she was rarely out of sight of the pair's future nesting place when the male was away.

Meanwhile nesting time had come for various other hole-nesting species of the neighbourhood, and they were all on the look out for suitable woodpecker holes. Tits, great tits in particular—take over woodpecker holes of every kind and these birds were now investigating the nesting hole that the great spotted woodpeckers had started whenever they were not about. However, these small creatures were no danger to the woodpeckers and offered no resistance when driven off by them.

Starlings have a preference for woodpecker holes, and with them it was quite another matter. A starling first turned up when tunnelling was in its third day and the work so far advanced that the hole and its entrance already offered attractive accommodation. The starling was immediately delighted with this new dwelling. A branch grew right by the side of it, not only making the approach easy but also allowing him to exhibit himself to his hen in a particularly striking way. Immediately after the inspection he put himself on guard and, ruffling his throat feathers, burst into song. The starling does not restrict himself to the trills of his own song but also imitates the calls of many other birds. So skilfully does he do so that in early spring one often scans the leafless treetops in the belief that an early golden oriole has arrived. Our starling spread his wings with a rowing movement every time another starling flew by. The resulting play of light on his iridescent shoulder feathers would, doubtless, draw attention to him from a passing hen or rival cock. Instead, however, the woodpecker returned from a foraging expedition, approaching so surprisingly fast that the starling took fright and flew off. Within ten yards the woodpecker had overtaken him and for a moment the two birds merged into a fluttering ball of feathers. They parted before hitting the ground, and the starling made off hastily, leaving our victorious woodpecker to carry on with his home building undisturbed.

Every day we saw cunning stratagems employed by usurpers to take over woodpecker holes. Five trees away a nuthatch had made its own nest in a great spotted woodpecker hole of the previous year. This strange bird is the only one which can run head first down a tree trunk just as quickly and easily as it can run up the trunk in the normal way. He is a regular inhabitant of woodpecker territories and so does not have very much difficulty in finding a suitable nesting hole left over from an earlier year.

37

The nuthatch's rivals are the starlings; and he would be powerless to protect his nesting place against enemies of their calibre were he not a particularly skilful builder. When he takes over a hole, the nuthatch starts collecting mud from a nearby puddle. He builds up this mud round the entrance to the hole, making it so small and narrow that while he can slip through it a starling cannot. This mud wall building takes a great deal of time and energy, especially when the starlings interfere with it.

Soon after the nuthatch had started on its wall a starling appeared at the hole. The reduced opening irked him so he began to pick it away, carrying off little crumbs of the drying mud in his beak. The nuthatch returned to find the intruder there and tried every possible way of driving the starling off. But what can a little fellow like a nuthatch do against a much stronger starling! Precious little, if it is merely a question of physical strength. So the nuthatch did not seek to prolong the open battle. He preferred to keep the starling off by continuing with his wall. As soon as the starling had left the tree the nuthatch threw himself furiously into his task. He reduced the entrance afresh and built new ramparts. Then the starling returned and immediately began breaking away pieces of them. As soon as he flew off with a beakful of mud, the nuthatch swung into action again. The battle lasted several days, but in the end the nuthatch won. Every day he made a little more progress and the ramparts grew thicker, as the starling could only peck away those parts of the entrance which were still damp. The lower parts of the wall had already dried hard. So the little nuthatch pair were able to keep their home and the starling had to move on elsewhere.

But to get back to our great spotted woodpeckers! For them, too, the struggle for existence was unremitting. From our hide we were observing the sixth day of nest-hole excavation; the hole was now about half way to completion, and the woodpecker was already working inside the tree trunk. After several bouts of hammering he would appear at the entrance and throw out the wood chips with a powerful swing of his beak.

He had just disappeared inside again when a starling alighted at the entrance to the hole. The woodpecker had heard him fly up, stood by and, as soon as the unsuspecting starling stuck its head into the hole, went over to the attack. The two birds became so entangled with each other that they fell to the ground. This time the starling did not take refuge in flight. With loud cries the two gave battle, pecking at each other and trying to get a grip with their claws. The struggle lasted for several seconds; we watched enthralled. Who would be the winner? Our interest was tinged with anxiety in case our woodpecker lost and we had to abandon our observation post and start all over again. Things looked bad for him. The woodpecker is not really at home on the ground. He is at his best among the trees where the shape of his feet and claws enables him to manoeuvre far more dexterously. Suddenly, however, he lunged at his opponent with his beak. He spread his tail wide on the ground to steady himself and brought his claws to bear. The starling reeled back and then fled. Our woodpecker had once again carried the day.

In general, woodpeckers need two or three weeks to complete their nesting holes. The rate of building naturally depends on how much help is given by the hen, whether the tree trunk is sound or rotten, and finally, on how far the season has advanced in the meantime. Nesting holes started later in the season are usually completed very fast. It took our woodpeckers twelve days to finish their hole in the birch tree. We congratulated ourselves because they had remained faithful to their nesting place, which could not have been more favourably sited for our observations and filming. This meant that we would be able to film the woodpeckers rearing their brood in the same place and in the same way as we had done while they were tunnelling. As it happened, though, we had congratulated ourselves too soon. When we went to inspect our woodpeckers' hole two days after it had been completed, we saw to our dismay a triumphant starling sitting on the branch by the entrance. The woodpecker had started building a new hole a hundred yards away. The new site was thirty-two feet up near a thick, sloping branch which was quite unsuited to our particular needs.

39

Intruding starlings also put a spoke in our wheel in another part of the forest some weeks later. At the edge of a fir plantation stood a tall beech, in which, over the years, the woodpeckers had made a series of nesting holes one above the other. The top one had been the home of a black woodpecker but was now inhabited by a stock-dove. Below this were three great spotted woodpecker holes, the middle one being actually occupied by a great spotted woodpecker pair, the other two by starlings.

Naturally, we wanted to observe this community more closely. Within a few days of our discovery we had built a hide in the fresh green branches of a larch. The birds were still sitting on their eggs, so all was peace. This situation changed drastically when the young hatched out. Their appearance was the signal for great excitement which was further heightened by the fact that the woodpeckers and the starlings had to feed their young at frequent intervals and were constantly crossing each others' paths on their foraging flights.

Despite strife and abuse the young were regularly fed during the first two days on which we kept watch. But when, after some unseasonable rainy days we returned a week later to film this strange colony, the starlings had also occupied the third hole. We waited in vain for our woodpeckers. Had the starlings used force, and thrown the young woodpeckers out of the nest? We searched the ground all round the tree several times, but found no trace of them. Probably the woodpeckers had not been able to stand the noisy starlings, who were in any case numerically superior, and had voluntarily relinquished their nesting site.

We had already shared the troubles and worries of the great spotted woodpeckers while they were preparing their nesting holes. Now we were curious to know how the powerful black woodpecker had fared against marauders and usurpers. Black woodpeckers prefer to tunnel out their nesting holes in tall trees on the edges of clearings. Their greatest preference is for beech trees, where they excavate immediately below the top.

In the middle of our woodpecker forest was a pine and larch copse which bordered on a beech plantation more than a hundred years old. Here

40

constant drumming could be heard, so from the middle of March onwards we set a watch in the shadow of the thickly-growing pines to observe the first phase of the black woodpeckers' building activities. Several times we saw how the male would select suitable nesting sites and offer them to the hen in a special ceremony. The first time this happened was on March 17th. The male flew up to a hole which had been only half finished the year before. Then he looked it over several times, glancing across at the hen as well. She had alighted on a neighbouring tree trunk, and he called to her with his two-syllable call of 'pee-ack', very much like that of the jackdaw. Anybody hearing this call in a forest can be certain that he has discovered a woodpecker pair in their breeding quarters. The call is heard from the beginning of pairing until the young leave the nest, particularly during the time when the eggs are being hatched, when it signifies 'relieve me on guard duty'.

When the hen did not respond to the male's invitation he began to tap with his beak in a special way. He held his body as when drumming, with neck drawn in and his beak very near the tree trunk. What was amazing was that he held his head back so far, and tapped so softly with his beak that it obviously had nothing to do with tunnelling or searching for food. It was a demonstrative expression of his wish to offer the hen a nesting place. When the male indulges in this gentle tapping he generally does it against the inside wall of the hole, inviting the hen to accept it as a nesting site.

During the following weeks and months we established that both the cock and the hen tapped in this way, and that they did so not only when selecting a nesting hole, but also during the incubation period and during the first phase of development of their young, whenever they relieved each other on guard duty.

Once we came across a black woodpecker male just beginning to chisel out a wedge from a tree. As the hen approached with loud cries of 'krri, krrri, krrri' the male bird flew a little way towards her and guided her to the chosen tree with 'jackdaw calls'. After the male had tapped on the trunk three times the hen alighted near him and began tunnelling immediately.

At a different nesting site a hawk came flying swiftly and silently by. Despite the warning messages of the starlings, finches, thrushes and tits which heralded the hawk's approach, the woodpecker—it was a hen—realised her danger only at the very last moment when she looked up after a burst of hammering. She just managed to dart round behind the tree in time. Had she tried to fly off, the hawk would certainly have caught her in a flash. She was visibly scared and as the hawk disappeared and the cries of warning in his wake grew fainter, she flew off screaming shrilly to give the alarm to the male. It took him a good quarter of an hour to bring his frightened mate back to the nesting site. He then flew up to the entrance hole and began hammering and the hen followed suit.

We noticed that the black woodpeckers, unlike the great spotted woodpeckers, shared the task of building a nesting hole equally. The finished hole of these big birds can be up to eighteen inches deep and ten inches in diameter, and it is practically impossible for one bird alone to hollow out a nesting hole of this size in a sound tree.

While it was the starlings which exploited the abundance of great spotted woodpecker holes, here it was the jackdaws who took possession. In this particular black woodpecker 'colony' we put their number at twenty pairs. This was in addition to some ten stock-dove pairs which had laid claim to other holes, so our woodpeckers suffered a great deal before being able to breed undisturbed.

At the beginning of April they decided to continue work on the half-finished hole; and from then on one or other of them was at work from morning till night. The urn-shaped hole was not yet deep or wide enough to allow the woodpeckers to work completely inside. They had to chisel away at the wood almost perpendicularly; and we could see their tails sticking out of the hole and jerking up and down. At this time any enemy whose attention was drawn from afar by the woodpeckers' hammering could easily have attacked them and done a great deal of harm, but the woodpeckers were obviously well aware of the danger. After every burst of hammering which could be anything from seven to twenty strokes they would pop out of the hole and have a good look round for several seconds. When they did this it was quite obvious that they were keeping an eye on the jackdaws. Most of the jackdaw pairs were already building their nests, and flew back and forth to the old beech trees in search of dry twigs which they took up in their beaks. But some of them were still wrangling over nesting sites, so it was inevitable that very soon a jackdaw appeared at our black woodpeckers' hole and indicated quite clearly that it was interested in the hole.

Something surprising now happened. The black woodpecker cock had taken over from the hen and had been hammering away for half an hour. He was still quite fresh, but was put completely off his stroke by the jackdaw which was perched some five yards away, and was staring at the hole. The woodpecker broke off his work at once, took cover behind the tree and examined the inquisitive visitor with outstretched head. Then the jackdaw, still some distance away and without attacking, gave his loud call of 'chak, chak'. The woodpecker abandoned his hole in a hurry; the jackdaw flew in to inspect it.

The hole was still unfinished, needing at least another ten days' work, but the jackdaw seemed quite satisfied with it as it was. After dodging in and out of the hole several times, he called his mate to him. It was clear that they intended to nest there because one of them was always in the neighbourhood from then on.

The woodpecker pair flew round and round the hole until evening. The cock finally grew so excited that he flew up to a drumming branch nearby and broke out into several bursts of drumming. This had not the slightest effect on the intruders. The woodpeckers did not attack them, and as there was obviously no other way of driving them off, the jackdaws began next day to build their nest in the hole.

When next morning we entered our hide by the tree where the nesting hole was, one of the jackdaws was peering out. After a few minutes the second one appeared, carrying some nesting material in its beak, and during the morning they took turns to fetch twigs for their nest. Two hours later, when both jackdaws were away from the hole at the same time, the woodpecker plucked up enough courage to fly up to his tree again. Even then he alighted not in his usual place at the entrance, but on the other side of the tree and six feet lower down. From there he looked round anxiously and, seeing no sign of the jackdaws, climbed very carefully up to the nest. He looked as if he had a bad conscience about being there at all, and behaved as if he would have to fly off any second because one of the new tenants would shortly be back.

When the woodpecker had reached the hole he made a quick preliminary inspection and then disappeared inside. Almost a minute later he reappeared, his beak crammed full of some of the jackdaws' nesting material. He bent his head sharply downwards and then swung it sharply upwards casting the offending material from him in a wide arc. He repeated these actions twice, but before he could empty the hole completely and continue with his tunnelling he heard the call of one of the jackdaws which was already in the neighbourhood.

We had supposed that the black woodpecker would defend his newly-regained home from the shelter of the hole. All he needed to do to keep the jackdaws off, was to stick his long beak out like a lance. Nothing of the kind happened. After another powerful call from the jackdaws the woodpecker cleared off without the slightest attempt at defence.

In the afternoon he began a new hole in a tree a hundred yards away, and worked there with his mate for two days. But he did not seem to like the place much. We saw him try again for a moment to win back his former nesting site. Once more he climbed up to the entrance, but this time he discovered that there had been a decisive development. The jackdaws had not only replaced the nesting material he had thrown out, but had already begun to lay their eggs. The woodpecker hurled one egg out of the hole; this happened so quickly that we were unable to photograph it. Then, of his own accord, he flew off without waiting for the jackdaws to return. He made no more attempts that spring to set up a home in that part of the forest.

I had several further occasions to observe this struggle between the black woodpeckers and the jackdaws in their search for a nesting place. I believe that most woodpeckers complete their nesting holes without disturbance only when the needs of intruders have been satisfied. One must beware, however, of looking at these happenings through human eyes—and therefore feeling sorry for the diligent woodpecker who so often works hard and long for the benefit of lazy good-for-nothings. The woodpeckers' urge to tunnel is a drive they have for only a limited time in the spring. Certainly, the achievements of these birds are astonishing; but we must not forget that they are specially equipped for making holes in tree trunks, and that they do this only within certain quite restricted limits.

As things turned out, it would hardly have been possible to film the most important phases of the black woodpeckers' tunnelling operations had not another pair started in a secluded part of the forest a long way from the jackdaws' habitat. They started work thirty-six feet from the ground. Unfortunately the site faced north, so we could only film successfully for about an hour in the early morning. As soon as the site became overshadowed by the trunk of the tree, we changed over from filming to sound recording. As had happened in earlier film work with wild animals, I managed to record not only the normal sounds connected with various activities, but also the many background noises which could be heard simultaneously.

When a film portrays an incident in nature, music is only a substitute for natural background sounds, and is in fact very often a disturbing factor. Furthermore, nature's sounds are not only essential components of a wild life film, but also heighten its atmosphere and authenticate it. We had built a complete sound recording studio in a trailer with its own supply of current. The trailer could be parked anywhere, whether near independent sources of electric current or not. We set up our recording equipment a hundred yards from the hole in a thick clump of young pine trees, and from there ran a cable to the woodpecker tree. It was not easy to instal the microphone where it would pick up the sounds we wanted, for the beech tree was more than a hundred years old and its trunk was almost three feet thick. This made it very difficult to climb, even with irons. We tried throwing a rope weighted with a hammer over a branch growing above the woodpecker hole; but each time the rope got entangled in neighbouring branches, so in the end we had to attempt the climb.

The best position for the microphone was some eight inches or so above the hole's entrance, behind the stump of a rotten branch. We had to secure it firmly to the tree so that it would not swing about in the wind and frighten the woodpeckers. George nailed a metal bracket to the trunk, and we could then raise the microphone into position whenever we wanted to.

A quarter of an hour after we had switched on the recording apparatus we heard the woodpeckers alighting. We had also connected a loudspeaker to the microphone so that we could control the volume and sound quality and also know exactly what was going on in the hole. The woodpecker noticed that there had been a change as soon as he arrived and climbed round and round the edge of the hole with little jumps, surveying this strange object near his home. The microphone was camouflaged with twigs, though we had left the aperture with the diaphragm uncovered so that it could pick up the sounds clearly. This gleaming silver spot on the microphone seemed to upset the woodpecker. After some delay he approached the microphone with quick little hops, and we lost no time in turning down the volume as we expected him to start pecking powerfully at the instrument. We could still remember the ear-splitting noise which had once arisen when a stag had found our microphone concealed at his rutting place, impaled it on his antlers and then dashed into the forest with the cable trailing behind him. But the woodpecker did nothing like that, however he inspected the microphone from all sides and then scrambled back to the hole and got on with his tunnelling.

After half an hour he was relieved by the hen with her 'jackdaw' cries and ceremonial tapping. We had thus managed in one fell swoop to record the most important sounds connected with nesting hole boring. But just as when we were filming, unfavourable circumstances created difficulties here. Our photographic failures were caused mostly by inadequate lighting conditions; a cloud would pass before the sun or a branch would obscure the hole at the very moment that something important was happening. With sound recording the trouble was extraneous noises like a dog barking, an aeroplane flying overhead, or worst of all, the noise of motors. The countryside is now so closely covered with motor roads that it is almost impossible to make good sound recordings of natural life without the intrusion of irrelevant noises. Wandering through a forest, armed only with binoculars, we do not notice these noises because we are now so used to them that our ears filter them out. With sound recording the position is quite different. The microphone is totally unselective and picks up all sounds within range. It would be sheer torture to listen to sound recordings of wild life if one was not able sometimes to make recordings almost uncluttered by extraneous noise where the voice of nature is heard clearly and without interference. Wind and rain can also render the sounds of nature almost unrecognisable, and sound recording impossible.

That is what happened to us on that first day. The wind made our recording useless. Weather conditions were the same the next day; and we could not film either as the sun was masked by clouds.

Only on the third day did the wind die down. Early in the morning, before the woodpeckers had arrived, we hoisted the microphone into position over the hole; and soon we were listening to the assiduous hammer blows of the woodpeckers as they carried on with their nest building.

Suddenly, when the woodpecker had been hammering for an hour without a break a second outburst of hammering assaulted our ears. George and I looked at each other questioningly. Had something gone wrong with our sound equipment? Perhaps it was an echo?

47

I tracked down the source of this new hammering through the pine trees, and was amazed to discover our cock woodpecker fifty yards away hard at work on another tree trunk. He had begun a new hole while the hen was still working away at the old one. We were fighting a losing battle, because we were almost convinced from previous experience that the cock would never return to the old site. The new site he had chosen seemed to him more suitable, for some reason, and sure enough in the afternoon the hen followed him.

This time, however, what we had regarded as an unfortunate mishap turned out to be just the opposite, because the new site was only twenty-one feet off the ground and faced south-west, giving excellent lighting conditions for filming.

A wealth of observation exists on the sites chosen by woodpeckers for their holes. Most of them face in a north-easterly to south-easterly direction, though a large percentage of woodpeckers prefer due north. It would seem that the woodpeckers prefer that side of the tree because it is the weather side and the bark there is at its roughest, affording the best grip for their climbing-iron claws. This is particularly true of the beech tree, at least until tunnelling has become so far advanced that the woodpecker can clamp himself to the edge of the hole. During the first phase of tunnelling, we often saw them slide on the bark as they alighted. It might be thought that the holes, being on the weather side, might be more vulnerable to storm and rain, but the woodpeckers take precautions against this. As we could see from our new hide, they incline the entrance steeply upwards inside the trunk.

The woodpecker excavates his urn-shaped nesting hole instinctively, automatically making it the correct shape and using the right methods. Nevertheless our indigenous species, whose building methods are to a large extent similar to each other, have developed different methods of chiselling out the entrance to their holes. Apart from the size, the shape of the hole also indicates which species has made it. The great spotted woodpecker makes his entrance hole almost circular. Green woodpeckers

48

From our hide we watched the latest happenings at the green woodpeckers' hole. Here the male is feeding a nestling

When already partly grown the young of the great spotted woodpecker were fed
from outside the nest: but the parent birds still climbed inside several times a day to clean it out

prefer an oval lying on its side, while the black woodpecker makes his entrance hole an upright oval. Woodpeckers seem to have a mechanical appreciation of the principles of architecture. In the same way that a diadem spider spins its perfectly proportioned web, or the reed-warbler builds its basket nest among the reeds without needing to learn the principles and technique of building, the woodpecker chisels away at a tree trunk until he achieves a perfectly-shaped nesting hole.

In the case of the three black woodpecker pairs we observed, the cock and hen divided the work almost equally between them. When tunnelling started they relieved each other surprisingly often. Thus on April 7th when they had moved to a new site and begun to work together, it looked as if they wanted to make up for lost time. In the course of one hour they changed over twelve times. Once they had got into the swing of tunnelling they usually changed over every forty to fifty minutes; but as with drumming, the weather affected the rate at which they worked. On stormy days the woodpeckers did not get much done because the wind caught their feathers and affected their balance, so they usually gave up after a short time.

On April 17th our woodpeckers had made such progress with their excavations that they were working deep inside the hole and invisible from outside. In this phase the birds needed less time for guard duties, and so the work went forward more quickly. We counted up to a hundred hammer blows a minute. Each burst of hammering comprised from five to seventeen strokes, and after four to eight minutes of hammering the woodpeckers stopped and threw the piles of wood chippings out of the hole. Their movements were quite different from those of the great spotted wood-pecker. The latter swung their heads to the right, while the black woodpeckers bent theirs downwards and then swung them sharply upwards (as we had seen in the incident with the jackdaws), thereby throwing the chippings straight up into the air. Each time the black woodpecker did this he put so much strength behind it that we gained the impression that he wanted to hurl the wood chips as far away as possible so that none

49

would fall at the foot of his tree and betray the whereabouts of his nesting hole. In windy weather the black woodpecker often succeeded in throwing them as far as twenty yards away. Usually however, despite all the birds' efforts, the wood chips accumulated at the bottom of the nesting tree, but by the time incubation began they were usually covered over by fresh green undergrowth.

On the fifteenth day of tunnelling, the cock had just thrown out a pile of wood chips and returned to his work inside the hole, when a jackdaw pair arrived and alighted at the entrance. Only one of them looked inside, and then they both made off hastily with such strident cries that I was convinced that the woodpecker had this time used his beak on them.

When work on the hole is so far advanced that there is enough room for the woodpecker inside it, the cock stays there overnight. This is the same with all woodpeckers, because the cock's urge to nest grows stronger than that of the hen, when the hole nears completion, and breeding begins. Perhaps the hen wishes to start building up her strength before the nest is finished, so that she will be at her best when the time for laying comes.

After twenty-one days of work, our woodpeckers' hole seemed to be ready, and they did only a little hammering now and then. They were obviously just smoothing the walls. From now on they never left their hole unoccupied if they could help it. Apparently laying starts during the last stages of smoothing the walls of the nesting hole, and one of the woodpeckers is always there to prevent an intruder from taking over their completed home at the last moment. Apart from jackdaws and stock-doves there are many other creatures which would find a woodpeckers' hole an ideal nesting site in late spring. Flycatchers, and in many places, golden-eyes, as well as animals like dormice, tree living bats and even squirrels with young to rear, can put woodpecker holes to good use. The woodpecker can best defend his home from the inside against these intruders. As we had seen on the last occasion when some jackdaws had attempted a take-over, the woodpecker's defence is outstandingly successful when nest

50

building is almost complete. And I think that a glimpse of his brightly coloured beak in the dim light of the hole has a demoralising effect on any intruder.

Like the nesting hole, the bed on which the eggs are laid is also a result of the woodpeckers' tunnelling. They do not bring material for the nest from outside, but lay their eggs on a bed of small wood chippings and wood waste which has collected during final tunnelling operations Numerous observations have shown that hen woodpeckers lay one egg a day, usually in the early morning. Most species lay from four to six, though the great spotted woodpecker quite often lays seven and the green woodpecker sometimes eight.

SIX

Inside a Nesting Hole

Ever since the woodpeckers had started tunnelling in earnest we had debated the best way of finding out what went on inside their nesting holes. Obviously we could not photograph through the tree trunk with X-rays, so the only way was to make a cut across the rear of the hole and replace the end wall with a pane of glass. In fact this meant cutting away about a quarter of the woodpeckers' nest; whether they would put up with the protracted work involved, and the alteration of their nesting hole (no matter how carefully we went about it), was—to put it mildly—a question! If the experiment were to have any chance of success we would have to choose between two methods of making the hide, each with its advantages and disadvantages.

If we were to erect a well-camouflaged hide like a hunting cabin no great changes would be necessary near the woodpecker tree. Depending on the behaviour of the birds, we would have either slowly to make an opening in the tree trunk and take our photographs from the hide through the window in the tree, or use the other method and build a hide right against the tree, making a cut across the end of the hole and sealing it off with the side walls of the hide. The hide would have to be absolutely dark inside, before the rear wall of the nest could be removed. It seemed most unlikely that the woodpeckers would then be able to see our 'photographic studio' in the darkness while we were observing what went on in their nest. Such little light as came in through the entrance hole in the tree trunk

52

would be enough for us to get our bearings. If we used the second type of hide we would (we hoped) be able to try out infra-red photography for the first time in nature film making.

Although the opening into the woodpeckers' nest would be made from within a darkened room, and it was unlikely that the infra-red light would frighten the birds, the first plan—of a hide three yards away—seemed to me to have a greater chance of success.

It seemed better to leave the more timid black and green woodpeckers alone and make our first attempt with the great spotted woodpeckers. We had often seen them in gardens and parks and knew that they were tamer than any of the other species. This encouraged us to try our luck.

Unfortunately, we had no success in our search for a suitable great spotted woodpecker hole. The birds whose work in the birch tree we had already recorded had made their nest hole near the top of an oak tree in one of the branches. A second pair had made theirs in a tree trunk only nine feet off the ground; but the tree was a perfect specimen which the forester would certainly not allow us to mutilate. We found a third nesting hole in an oak tree three feet thick; but here it would have been almost impossible to cut through to the nest.

Those who plan nature films to cover a complete year of wild life activity, must hedge their bets; so we had chosen the Favorit Park, Ludwigsburg near Stuttgart, as the second string to our bow. We had already visited that area in February and found many great spotted woodpeckers among its ancient oaks. However, because there are no black woodpeckers, in which we were particularly interested, in the Favorit Park, we decided to work in the Dülmen Forest. Moreover, I had film work to do at the Max Planck Institute of Comparative Physiology in Buldern which is near Dülmen. Dr. Löhrl, however, the director of the Ludwigsburg bird sanctuary, had promised to find me a large number of occupied holes if my search in the Dülmen forest should fail.

It was the beginning of May when we arrived in Ludwigsburg. The climate is milder there than in Dülmen, and breeding starts earlier, so the

53

young woodpeckers could already be heard crying for food from most of the nesting holes. Judging from the strength of the cries, some of them were almost full grown. When Dr. Löhrl conducted us round the great park of the palace to show us the holes he had marked out for us, we saw that more woodpeckers were in residence than we ever expected; yet not a single nesting hole complied with our exacting demands. There was no point in searching laboriously through the whole park for a nesting hole which might perhaps be suitable, when those we had seen already contained young so far grown. It looked as if we had lost the race against time to film the year's happenings in a woodpecker colony. We were resigned to writing off a year's work when at the last moment we had a stroke of luck—we found a suitable nesting hole.

We had already made plans to return to Dülmen; but before leaving George and I walked through the park, taking a last look at every hole and its occupants. In spite of all our past disappointments I still had a hunch that we might still find a nesting hole with a late brood here. As we inspected every tree trunk from all sides we discovered holes we had not known about before. Most of them were occupied by pied flycatchers, and others by starlings, great tits, blue tits, and nuthatches. Until we visited Ludwigsburg I had had no idea of the important part woodpecker holes played in the life of these small birds.

To identify the occupants of the holes we scraped a long stick against the bark of the tree, moving it slowly nearer to the mouth of the hole. If we had tapped on the tree the reaction of many occupants of these holes would have been to sit even closer to their brood. But by merely scratching softly, we aroused their curiosity. They probably thought an intruder was near and left their brood to see.

We had already examined more than a hundred tree trunks with this technique and were using it on a wild cherry tree when a woodpecker flew out. He was so agitated that there must have been either a clutch of eggs or a young brood in his hole. The angry cock (for such he was) gave vent to a prolonged 'kik, kik, kik, kik', and was immediately joined by the hen.

54

We drew back hastily so that we could watch the woodpeckers and find out from their behaviour which phase they had reached. We had just hidden behind a bush when the male bird returned and disappeared into the hole. In the course of an hour the pair relieved each other three times. After ten minutes the hen appeared, and forty minutes later the male returned. Through powerful binoculars I could see that they were not bringing food. This meant that the young had not yet hatched out. Our thankfulness was increased by the fact that the hole was not more than twelve feet from the ground. At that point the wild cherry was only ten inches thick and was not a particularly good specimen, being neither upright nor with masses of foliage. We hoped therefore that we should be allowed to carry out our plans for photographing the inside of a woodpecker's hole.

That afternoon the officials of the Park administration inspected the tree and, naturally enough, wanted to be told every detail of what we planned to do. They were doubtful of our success but agreed to let us try. The same afternoon we began gradually to accustom the woodpeckers to our working methods, and sawed off the top of the tree from a point nine feet above their hole. Great spotted woodpecker holes are six to seven inches across and up to twelve inches high. We had to saw off the top of the tree because opening up the woodpecker hole would so weaken it that a strong wind could snap it off just at the hole. We did not want to keep the woodpeckers away from their quarters for too long, so we worked from tall ladders, using a two-handed saw. Although we did not have much freedom of movement, the saw bit quickly into the wood; and after twenty minutes we were able to fasten a rope to the tree top and pull it down.

During this operation the woodpeckers flew round us uttering loud warning cries. The longer we kept them away from their nest, the bolder they grew and the closer they approached. We could not keep them away from the tree top and they were actually sitting there when we pulled it down. This frightened them so much that they made off at speed.

Their nesting site had now changed appreciably from a shady tree to a naked trunk nineteen feet high and bathed in sunlight. The two forestry workers who had helped us fell the top of the tree shook their heads doubtfully when they looked up at the hole. They thought that the woodpeckers might get over the fright they had had, but there would certainly be trouble if we sawed away the end of their nest—even if we took all day to do it. In fact, they were sure that the birds would abandon their nesting hole completely.

The forestry workers had barely had time to leave when the woodpeckers reappeared. They flew round their nesting place for a few minutes to take stock of the altered situation and then the male alighted at the entrance to the hole and disappeared inside. The hen stayed noisily in the entrance for a while and then flew off in search of food. When she returned half an hour later and called to the male bird, 'toowit, toowate', signifying her willingness to take over sitting on the eggs, we knew that the first part of our plan had succeeded.

For the rest of the day we left the birds in peace. We kept an eye on the hole from a distance and at the same time went over our plans again. We decided to leave untouched the side of the tree with the entrance to the hole and to open up the nest as nearly vertically as possible from the rear—because three yards away there was a young beech which offered good possibilities for building a hide.

The next morning brought mild, sunny spring weather. We could not have wished for better. When we arrived at six o'clock the woodpeckers were sitting on the eggs; and we left them alone for two hours to follow their daily routine before we started work on the tree trunk.

From the photographic point of view it was important to ensure that the cut across the end of the nest should be vertical. This would make the urn-shape of the nest quite clearly visible from the hide and would permit the glass to be pushed squarely home against the rear of the nest. The best way to do this was to use a narrow-bladed saw to make a horizontal cut in the tree trunk and then to turn the blade and saw

56

In the black woodpeckers' territory.
These big birds, the size
of a crow, prefer to make their homes
in old beech trees
on the edges of clearings

All day we waited in vain, with our
telescopic camera at the ready,
for a chance of filming
the mating ritual of the shy
black woodpeckers

The black woodpeckers' changeover ceremony during nesting excavation

After the male has been hammering for fifty minutes without a pause he gives his two-syllable call of 'kleea' to indicate that he wants to be relieved

When his partner approaches he begins tapping at the edge of the hole with his beak, inviting the hen to take over . . .

. . . and before relinquishing the hole to the hen he taps again a few more times in the same fashion

When the woodpeckers
were working inside
the tree, they would
break off every four
to eight minutes to throw
out the wood chips
which had accumulated
in the hole

As soon as the black
woodpeckers' nesting holes
have reached habitable
size, the jackdaws begin to
take an interest in them

The big woodpeckers
abandon their holes
without any opposition
and let the jackdaws
usurp them

The black woodpecker did not object
to a microphone close
to the entrance to his hole

We had set up our 'sound studio',
camouflaged by a fir copse, a hundred
yards from the woodpeckers' home,
to make tape recordings
of the sounds at the nesting hole

perpendicularly downwards. When we started we soon found that we had chosen the most laborious and time consuming method. The thin blade took a long time to bite into the tree and when we started to saw downwards, jammed hard in the tough cherry wood, we had to make several wedge shaped cuts to release it. We did not work for more than twenty minutes, not long enough for the eggs to run any risk of damage in that mild weather. After a pause of one and a half hours we started again, timing our start for the moment when the returning woodpecker called his sitting mate out of the hole in order to relieve her.

We thought it advisable not to saw out the complete rear wall of the hole. Instead we removed four-inch strips, one at a time. This enabled us to use a more powerful saw after we had cut out the first strip, but even then it took us five hours, and it was six o'clock in the evening by the time we had finished. We had nailed the strips of wood back into position and filled up the chinks with moss so that the woodpeckers would not notice anything amiss when they returned and would enter their nest without any hesitation.

Before leaving our woodpeckers for the evening, we cut some cardboard to the shape of the opening we were making in the nest and used it as a template for the glass pane which was to serve as our window into the woodpeckers' dwelling.

We would see next morning whether the woodpeckers would tolerate the first noticeable alterations to the inside of their nest. When we pushed home the glass it would decrease the size of the hole by a third. Also, the birds were used to climbing up that part of the wall where the glass would be. If they tried to climb up when the glass was in position they would certainly skid and damage the eggs.

To prevent rattling and keep out draughts we puttied the glass all round and covered it with the original bark for the first phase of our operations. When the rear of the hole had been closed up again we took up a position behind a bush fifty yards away and waited tensely for the woodpeckers to return. The hen was the first to alight at the hole. She

57

ducked her head inside and then out again and repeated this several times. In the dim twilight inside the hole she had certainly been able to see that there had been some change, because she twice circled the trunk agitatedly and inspected the hole from all angles. She then called to her mate and both birds looked unbelievingly at the changed interior of their nest. This inspection lasted only three minutes and then the hen disappeared into the hole. She did not, as we had feared she might, skid on the glass and flee in a panic. Instead, after a few minutes, we heard a steady, light tapping. The hen was testing the glass with her beak, but it was much too thick for her to break. When we saw that the first stage of our project had succeeded and that the woodpeckers were again sitting on their eggs, we left them alone for three hours. Then we started on the next stage— removing the protective covering of bark from the glass.

Our hopes for success were founded on the fact that woodpeckers' nesting holes are not dark all the time nor yet in continuous twilight. The amount of light coming through the entrance hole varies with the time of day, and in the early morning, for instance, sunbeams shine directly into the entrance for a short time. That is why I thought it quite possible that the woodpeckers would become accustomed to light entering their nest from the rear as well as from the front.

We next sawed off enough wood from the pieces we had nailed back, for a shaft of light three quarters of an inch wide to shine through the upper edge of the glass. However, the rear of the nest was so obscured by foliage that the birds took little notice of the change and by the evening we had removed almost half the rear wall.

It was important that we should have the nesting site under continuous observation to note the effect of our experiment on the woodpeckers' behaviour, so we divided the work. I stayed with the woodpeckers —but at a distance of a hundred yards to avoid disturbing them. George built the hide with the assistance of one of the forestry workers. It was a kind of hunting cabin and its height had been carefully worked out to allow the camera to be set up at the level of the woodpecker hole. We used dry

58

pine branches and planks; and the hide was so light that we were able to move it bodily into position. The thick foliage of the young beech three yards from the hole served to camouflage our hide. We then covered it with canvas and concealed it under a mound of beech and pine branches. To ensure that it would not collapse in stormy weather we supported the uprights with a number of thick poles, and these were in turn held upright by the neighbouring trees.

None of this disturbed the great spotted woodpeckers in the least; all the same, we kept watch on them until the rays of the setting sun were reflected from the upper half of the glass at the back of their nesting hole where we knew that the male bird was sitting on the eggs. Toads were croaking their nuptial song in the ditches, a nightingale was singing its evening theme by the pool, and then a thrush fluttered up to its rostrum at the top of a fir tree, singing away joyfully as the sky grew pale.

It was an enchanting end to a day which had seen our dreams begin to come true. We had had many disappointments, but in two more days we hoped to lay bare the secrets of the woodpeckers' nest. The following day we were to discover how easily wild creatures can upset calculations of that kind.

Next day the woodpeckers let us remove two thirds of the back wall of their nest by noon. We did so in two stages, and both times the birds continued sitting on the eggs. It seemed as if the woodpeckers were now so used to having part of their nest missing that we could safely remove the last third of it. This last third, the party wall dividing the broody bird from the outer world, was, however, to be our undoing.

When we removed the last section of the wall at about three in the afternoon the birds became extremely agitated. They climbed about the hole for some seconds, their behaviour showing that their patience was at an end. In the hope that they would calm down and continue sitting on their eggs, we had intended to leave them for a quarter of an hour, when there was a totally unexpected development. The hen bird started hammering at the floor of the nesting hole with the apparent object of making

59

it much deeper. Even after throwing out five lots of wood chips she was still hammering away; we thought it was high time she stopped, because the eggs were in danger of being damaged.

The woodpeckers' reactions forced us to give in. With heavy hearts we closed up the hole again hoping that by using the same methods we should at least be able to watch the rearing of the young in the hole. This was more important that observing the hatching of the eggs.

When the nesting hole had been restored to its former state, the birds resumed their incubation of the eggs, and after three days of keeping watch we knew that an important change had taken place.

The woodpeckers stayed in the hole only a few minutes at a time and both of them stayed away for increasingly long periods. Something decisive must have happened. No young could have been hatched, for if they had, the birds would not both have been absent from the nesting place for long periods at a stretch, and at least one of them would have appeared with the first meal for their young. We listened carefully outside the nest for the rasping cries with which woodpecker young announce their arrival soon after they have hatched. We heard nothing.

The next day we saw that the woodpeckers were spending very little time in their hole, so we called Dr. Löhrl into consultation and then decided to have a look at the eggs. We found that there were no signs of embryonic development and that the eggs were not even fertilised.

This was a painful discovery, because the year was now so far advanced as to rule out any possibility of finding a new nest with unhatched eggs in it. But then I began to think that there was after all a possibility of continuing our work with the same woodpecker pair at the same nesting hole, even though they had already cost us so much time and unrewarded effort. We would try an experiment and see whether our woodpeckers would adopt a strange brood. During the past few days we had heard what were obviously newly hatched young birds clamouring for food. The nesting hole was thirty feet above the ground, in a tree trunk so thick that we could never have opened it up for photography. In any case the tree was commercially valuable, so it was doubtful whether we would have received permission even if it had been possible to open it up. There was no opposition to my plan to remove the young and everyone in the bird sanctuary thought it feasible.

There were five unfledged young woodpeckers in the hole. They were three days old, and might have been put there specially for our purpose. We wanted to carry out our experiment using two of them at a time, since in pairs they can keep each other warm, whereas singly they cannot.

The hide was three hundred yards away and while we made our way to it I held the naked youngsters in my armpits to keep them warm, since we were afraid that the woodpeckers would not return soon enough to take the youngsters under their protection. It was easy to take off the glass and its wooden covering, so the move to new quarters was quickly accomplished. We had not even removed the ladder from against the tree when the male woodpecker alighted on a nearby tree and uttered his sharp warning cry of 'Kix, kix, kix, kix'. We withdrew as quickly as possible, and the woodpecker flew up to the hole and immediately disappeared inside. We waited tensely to see what his reaction would be. That he did not immediately reappear was encouraging. Ten minutes later he flew hurriedly away. When he returned with the hen we could clearly see that he had food in his beak.

Half an hour later the parents were feeding their adopted brood with such energy that we confidently expected to be able to introduce a third youngster into the hole. We had to do this because a group of at least three young was necessary to obtain exact observations of woodpecker behaviour inside their nesting holes. Of course, we were sorry to have to deprive the natural parents of three of their young. But it is a mistake to attribute human feelings to woodpeckers. Where human parents will lavish extra love and attention on a weak or sick child, for instance, woodpeckers just leave such a youngster to its fate. With birds, feeding of their young is a compulsive urge so the ones which stretch out their beaks furthest are fed first. Thus the weaklings are easily neglected and die off

61

to be thrown out of the nest by the parent birds without the least compunction. As we had left the other woodpeckers two youngsters, they would still be able to fulfill their instinct to rear a brood.

Until evening our woodpeckers fed the young regularly and conscientiously just as we had seen other woodpeckers do. Food there was in plenty, thanks to the dry, warm weather. The larvae of the green bell moth had hatched out and were hanging in masses from the tree trunks. All our woodpeckers needed to do was to pick them off, and every three to five minutes one of them would return to the nest with its beak crammed full.

Since woodpeckers grow quickly and we wanted to observe them while they were still unfledged we made all haste with our final preparations for photography. It was as easy as it had been during the incubation period to take away part of the rear wall of the hole as long as the woodpeckers could take cover at the bottom. When we uncovered all the glass, the woodpecker again began to chisel away the floor of the nesting hole. This time it was the male which did the chiselling. As soon as we covered the glass with beech leaves he stopped, and both woodpeckers resumed their normal feeding rhythm. We allowed the leaves to wither, in this way letting more light into the hole, and later we were able to take them away without the woodpeckers seeming to notice.

Despite the opening we had made in the hole, too little light entered it for us to be able to make any films under normal conditions. So to light the nest we mounted three 1000-watt spotlights on the roof of our hide and camouflaged them with beech branches. We obtained electric current from the forestry workers' building two hundred yards away.

On May 15th our preparations were complete and we were ready for the last and most critical phase of our operations: accustoming the woodpeckers to the glare of the spotlights. We waited till the sun rose over the tree tops behind our hide and shone straight into the entrance of the hole. When we switched on the first spotlight and trained it on the nesting hole, we saw to our delighted amazement that the woodpeckers were not particularly perturbed by it.

Shortly before the birds returned from their next foraging flight we switched on the second spot and then the third. The woodpeckers returned and looked after their young with their usual devotion. Success at last! We could go ahead with our film work. At ten o'clock in the morning of May 16th we set up the camera on its tripod and made ready telescopic lenses, reels of film and accumulators. We checked the camouflage of the hide from every direction; and then George walked off, followed by the woodpeckers. We had arranged that I would hang a white cloth from the rear of the hide as a signal whenever I saw something unusual happening. He, meanwhile, would keep the hide under observation from a distance and relieve me after seven hours. When working close to a nest it is at all costs essential to avoid entering the hide unaccompanied. Should one do so it is very likely that the birds will either cease to behave naturally or will abandon their nest, even though they may, till then, have so far seemed to be accustomed to the presence of the hide. But if, however, two people enter the hide together and one then makes off very quickly, the birds do not realise that there is someone left in the hide. They have seen a human being approach and then go away, so they return unconcernedly to their nests.

These tactics had been thoroughly tried out on many occasions in the past and we now put them into operation again. George had been gone only a few minutes when the hen flew up to the entrance of the nest. I waited tensely to see what would happen inside it.

The very first feed yielded observations which more than compensated for all the effort and disappointments of the last weeks. The woodpecker called to its mate twice, using the special call which signified that she had arrived to relieve him. The young took no notice at all, and in fact the hen had made the calls from habit to announce her arrival in case the male should be within on guard. The woodpecker had just entered the hole when I saw that she was climbing about inside the tree trunk in a hitherto unobserved manner. As I pointed out earlier in the book only the nuthatch can descend a tree head first, and it does so with as little effort as when it is climbing in the usual way. Woodpeckers, however, which spend almost their entire lives climbing about, are seen only with their heads erect. When they hop downwards they do so holding their bodies upright, because their feet and leg muscles are not strong enough for them to be able to climb about without using their tail for support. But inside its hole the woodpecker can descend head first because the urn-shaped nest is so narrow. By spreading its feet wide apart it can press them against the sides of the nest gaining extra support in this way. Our woodpeckers almost always entered their holes in this fashion, only rarely descending with their heads held upright. This habit of descending head first had many advantages when feeding the young, as I was soon to realise.

Woodpecker eggs hatch after twelve days and the young are born blind and naked. At birth they weigh less than a third of an ounce. Since the parents do not employ any sort of nesting material, the nesting hole with its floor covering of chippings and wood waste is not very warm. The young, with their tender, rosy skins, huddle together in a pyramid for warmth, necks outstretched. For the first few days their ear openings and eyes are closed. Unlike other hole-nesting species the parents do not announce feeding times with special calls or movements or by touching their young caressingly. Woodpeckers get their young to stretch themselves, hold up their heads and open their beaks by tapping lightly on the nodes on the sides of their beaks, which is the only way to elicit any response. The ability to be able to manoeuvre head down inside the nest is a definite advantage to the woodpecker, because it can then stretch out its beak like a finger and tap on the nestlings' beak nodes, and also because it can see better in the dim light from the entrance than if it had to feed the young over its shoulder.

Observation of the woodpeckers in their hole increased my wonderment at the versatility of their beaks. Outside their holes woodpeckers use their beaks for drumming, tapping on trees when displaying and searching for food. Inside their holes woodpeckers use them to feed their young and for scavenging the nest. When the young have been fed, the woodpeckers nudge the youngsters' rumps with their beaks. This makes them excrete and the parents immediately pick up the droppings in their beaks and fly off to get rid of them.

As soon as the youngsters were satisfied they would draw in their necks. They were at this stage still too weak to be able to hold their heavy heads upright. I noticed that if one of the young was somehow pushed apart from the group it would rest its head on the floor of the nesting hole; it made every effort to rejoin its companions in the warm huddle of the pyramid where it could rest its head on the back of the others. Sitting as they were on the rough surface provided by the scattering of wood chips on the bottom of the nesting hole, the young would certainly have been scratched but for the thick, rough, wart-like growths that protected their hindquarters like cushions.

There was so much going on in the hole that my seven hours' stint passed all too quickly although I could not film what I saw because I realised that the strong reflection of daylight on the glass would have caused white patches on the film, even when clouds passed across the sun. All the same, I was pleased. Behind the glass the birds were behaving quite naturally and were not at all perturbed either by the glass or by the lamps. Now all that had to be done was to keep out direct daylight. When George relieved me at five o'clock we nailed two posts to the roof of our 'film studio' and fastened them to the woodpecker tree a good three feet above the glass. We then spread some canvas across them to keep out the daylight without interfering with the beams of our spotlights. We hoped that the woodpeckers would not be frightened off by the change, but to make sure, we obscured the pane of glass for the night with leafy twigs so that there would be enough darkness for the male bird which usually spent the night keeping the young warm.

That evening in the forester's cottage we spent a long time discussing the many events of the day and completing our plans for the following day. We were very keyed up, for it was unusually exciting to think that we might well succeed in our attempts. Not only had we managed to

E

watch many intimate activities normally hidden from the observer, but we might even be able to record them on film. For nights past I had dreamt about all sorts of accidents which could have befallen the woodpeckers. Wild cats, martens or even owls might come across the nesting hole, and even if the glass held against their attacks, they might frighten the male bird away, leaving the defenceless nestlings to fall prey to the coldness of the night. Every morning at the earliest possible moment I hurried over to the nesting hole to see that everything was all right. That first night I would have camped out in the open and kept guard over the nest, but it was dark and pouring with rain, so the woodpeckers were not in any great danger. Well before day broke and the first light of dawn woke the sleeping forest, I was outside again to see how our woodpeckers started their day's work. I had to wait for three quarters of an hour. Most of the other birds had already started their dawn chorus when the hen wood-pecker swooped down to the hole. She had to sound her call and poke her head into the entrance several times before the male emerged. Then I heard the cries of the brood and knew that all was well.

As usual we let two hours go by because we did not want to transfer our equipment to the hide until the day had grown warmer and the young woodpeckers had been fed several times. It took twenty minutes to prepare everything and during this time the youngsters would have to manage without their parents.

At half-past eight George left me for another part of the park to continue filming starlings and nuthatches who were using woodpecker holes as nests. We were not far away from each other, so he could easily keep check on whether the white cloth was visible at the back of our 'studio', showing that something had happened. Five minutes after George had left, the male woodpecker returned with a beak full of food. I had already fitted a lens with a focal length of 300 millimetres, and this showed him clearly in the view-finder, making observation easier than with the naked eye. When the hen arrived I still did not start filming, but I had switched on the lights and observed the birds' reaction to them.

66

Once I had seen that the woodpeckers' activities were following their normal rhythm, as they had on the previous day, I concentrated my attention on the entrance to the nest. The arrival there of one of the woodpeckers would be the signal for my camera to start turning for the first time. Because of the narrow field of the lens everything depended on my picking up the woodpecker during its swift approach towards the entrance to the hole and then keeping pace with it. The lights had already been switched on when the hen made her appearance and the moment the tip of her beak approached the hole I started the camera turning. Many feet of valuable film were lost, however, because the bird did not enter the hole but merely peered inside several times and then flew away. I had thought that the pane of glass and the walls of the hide would deaden the sound of the camera, but I had reckoned without the woodpeckers' keen sense of hearing. The strange whirring noise disturbed the hen so much that she wheeled towards the hide to look for it and landed right on the roof. From there she went on looking. As I did not want to lose any more photographic material I resorted to a device which should always be tried when filming wild life. I took out the reel of film, covered the camera, and let it run without any film for the next three feeding times. The woodpeckers soon grew accustomed to the camera's monotonous whirring and resumed their normal activities.

With large birds which feed their young at infrequent intervals much time is usually needed to accustom them to the sound of the camera, but with these woodpeckers I had noted thirty-four feeding times in seven hours on the previous day. The rate was not much slower on this occasion, one of the woodpeckers appearing with its beak full of food every seven minutes or so. At this stage of the brood's development the woodpeckers shared the task of feeding about equally between them.

That day I spent eleven hours with the woodpeckers and was able to observe their habits closely. I discovered that feeding reached a climax in the morning, decreased somewhat in frequency at midday and increased again in the afternoon to about the same level as in the morning. This left the parents little time for keeping their brood warm, but while feeding them the parents often took the opportunity of enveloping the young in the warmth of their feathers, particularly in the early morning when the chill of night still lingered in the shadowy plantation. When one of the parents was warming the nestlings they would keep up a soft, nasal whimpering, just as they did while asleep in their pyramid. While the parents were out foraging, and even during feeding, at least one of the youngsters would keep up a constant clamour for food. This was a not very tuneful rhythmic burbling, interrupted every so often by four or five loud cries which sounded like ' gay, gay, gay, gay' and could be heard at quite a distance from the hole.

Once, when the parents had been absent from the nest for a longer time than usual, I saw one of the youngsters tap the floor with his as yet undeveloped beak, making a very weak first attempt to search for food in the wood of the nesting hole floor. The four-day old little bird hammered at the wood chippings several times, put out his tongue in the way a grown woodpecker does to trap insects, swallowing some little particles of wood in the process. I found this of particular interest because it showed how very early the woodpecker's co-ordination of tongue and beak develops.

The camera had recorded all this as well as everything that had been going on while the young woodpeckers were being fed. By the time George came to relieve me at seven o'clock I had used up all the film. Soon we were waiting excitedly for prints. When they are projected it is easy to judge their effectiveness but to check details of lighting and definition, contact prints are necessary. We could be well pleased with the results on this occasion. We had managed to achieve our first objective of filming the behaviour of the blind nestlings inside the nesting hole. We had three days left before the next stage of their development; when seven days old their eyes would open and we could start filming their behaviour in these new conditions. Meanwhile we intended to continue our observation of other birds which had taken over woodpecker nesting holes.

Nine miles or so from Ludwigsburg we had discovered a hoopoe pair occupying a green woodpeckers' hole in a cherry tree. The branches were so spreading and the foliage so thick that no sunlight reached the entrance to the hole at all. As the tree was thickly laden with ripe cherries we had a long talk with the tree's owner before he would agree to our sawing off several big branches to let in enough light for our film work!

These negotiations had been concluded some days ago. Then the branches had been removed and a small hide built close to the hoopoes' nesting place. We could now start filming, but as luck would have it we came on a day when the young hoopoes were preparing to leave the hole and so were being fed infrequently. Only twice did I see the parents fly up to the nest and offer some grubs, holding them out to the fledglings in their long curved, pincer-like beaks. The first feeding time was shortly after sunrise when there was not enough light for photography. At eight o'clock the first youngster flew off. Immediately afterwards a second young hoopoe appeared at the entrance to the hole, gathering courage for its first leap to freedom. The youngster stood there hesitantly, for some moments peering out of the hole while the rest of the brood waited impatiently. Then he drew back. This behaviour made it difficult to judge when the youngster would actually fly off. Several times I tried to film the young hoopoes as they left the nest one by one, but without success. Finally only one remained. With him I succeeded, however; and I obtained a number of shots of his parents feeding him and of him leaving the nest.

When we returned to our Ludwigsburg retreat at midday we went along to our woodpecker hole to see that everything was all right. We waited, but half an hour went by without either of the parent woodpeckers putting in an appearance. Then I noticed that the canvas had been torn away from its frame and was hanging slackly down against the tree. With angry foreboding we went to bring the ladders which we had hidden twenty yards away. When I had climbed up and taken away the twigs from the glass I saw the young woodpeckers lying in the nest in cramped, unnatural attitudes. There was no trace of the parents. As quickly as I could I unfastened the glass and put my hand inside the nest. The little bodies were cold, and when I picked them up there was no longer any doubt. They were dead. In all my nature studies few things had moved me as much as the sad end which had overtaken the young woodpeckers. George and I tried to think how it could have happened and suddenly remembered the storm of the night before. That was when the canvas came down, and its flapping against the glass must have scared the male woodpecker out of the nesting hole. He had been unable to find his way back to the nest in the darkness and so the unattended youngsters had died of cold.

We were upset by the sad fate of our young woodpeckers, but we would have to try to get the parents to adopt some more of the same age, otherwise we could not continue with our film work. It was more than likely that the woodpeckers had visited the nest between sunrise and noon and had decided that it would be useless to return any more. The chance of success was therefore a slim one, but we wanted to make the attempt just the same. As we had already found another hole with young woodpeckers in it, we set out without delay.

Getting the young out of the nest was going to be a ticklish job. The hole was thirty-six feet up in an oak tree and the entrance was below an almost horizontal branch which was so weathered that it would hardly take a man's weight. It was a really courageous feat when George looped a safety belt over the branch three yards from the trunk, wriggled along to the hole and started chipping away at the entrance with a hammer and chisel.

After thirty anxious minutes he managed to reach into the hole and bring out three young birds which he placed in a linen pouch. From his expression I knew straightaway that having once seen them he did not consider the youngsters really suitable for our purpose. When I opened the pouch I saw why. Not only were their eyes already open, but they also had feathers. I estimated their age at fourteen days. It was highly questionable whether they would be able to adapt themselves to the nesting hole with one wall missing and spotlights trained on it. Furthermore, the adult birds would be expecting naked, five-day old young. If they were to return and find these big feathered youngsters there, they were quite likely to regard them as intruders who had taken over the nest. However, we decided to try the experiment.

By the time we had transferred the fledglings and replaced the glass over the hole it was one o'clock. Neither of the woodpeckers had yet appeared, and we awaited them anxiously.

After an hour, during which the young woodpeckers had been crying out with increasing vigour for their step-parents, the male flew up to the hole. He looked inside the nest and then flew away again without having entered it at all. We hoped that he had gone to forage for food, but when he returned after half an hour his beak was empty. He did not go inside the hole but perched for a while a little way below it and then disappeared into the forest again for a long time.

My hopes began to dwindle. At three o'clock George reminded me that we had eaten nothing since four that morning. It would be all right to leave our post for a while because we could not influence events at the nesting hole in any case.

We returned at five o'clock and had a wonderful surprise. Just as we got there a woodpecker flew up with food in its beak. It entered the nest and shortly afterwards reappeared with droppings. Our woodpeckers had after all adopted the two-week old youngsters. We could continue with our work. The difference in age between the first and second broods meant that we had to amend our original plan of filming every stage in the development of the young woodpeckers.

At fourteen days old the young had all their plumage except for the tail and wing feathers which were still growing thickly. Their feet and claws had grown quickly from the very beginning and were now almost as well-developed as an adult bird's. Although their half-grown tail feathers did not provide them with any support, they had already started climbing.

71

They knew that the parent birds arrived at the entrance to the hole with food, and that the first one there to meet them was fed first.

When the parents were absent from the nest for longish periods, the youngsters would try out their climbing-iron claws. At first they often tumbled back into the nest, which led to squabbling amongst them. Heinroth considers woodpeckers to be such out-and-out individualists that even at breeding time, when they have to work together, they give the impression of grudging one another his or her share of looking after the brood, and there are frequent squabbles. We had not seen any squabbles of this kind between our woodpecker parents, although I had seen the male force his way into the hole when the hen had not responded to his offers to relieve her on duty. There had not been any fighting between them, though there might well have been in such a situation.

The behaviour of the youngsters among themselves was quite different. The stronger they became, and the more adept they became at climbing about the nest with claws and tail, the more their rivalry increased. When they were still very young they had huddled together for warmth, but now they turned their backs on each other. They were no longer dependent on one another and did not stay on the floor of the nest. Instead they hung by their claws from its sides. From these vantage points they uttered furious cries for food and raced towards the entrance whenever they heard one of the parent birds alighting. If two ravenous youngsters reached the entrance simultaneously a furious fight would break out, and they would hack at each other's heads with their beaks so viciously that I wondered how they managed to survive. When one of the contestants felt that he was losing and that the pace was growing too hot for him he would clamber out of reach.

I have rarely seen a defeated youngster pursued or attacked inside the nest itself. In only one of the nine nesting holes I inspected did I find a young woodpecker (twelve days old) which had died from pecks in the head. To my amazement, in the nest I was studying it was not the strongest of the three young woodpeckers who ruled the roost but the

72

The cooing of a stock-dove can be heard from a nearby hole.
These birds also use an old black woodpecker hole for their nesting site

With the help of climbing-irons we were able to reach every black woodpecker hole.
Most of them were more than thirty feet up, too high for us to build a hide near them

At last we had the luck to find a black
woodpecker hole only twenty-two feet up.
Working from a platform we opened
up the nest from the rear . . .

. . . and at the same time began building
our film studio which was to enclose the
opening in the tree-trunk completely

The experiment has been
successful. The hide was completed
in time for the hatching
of the young woodpeckers;
we covered it with tar paper
to waterproof it and keep
out the light

When our observations started
there was only a dim light,
filtering through from the entrance
to the nesting hole, to enable
us to see what was going on

smallest and least well-developed. For feeding at the entrance to the hole the young birds developed a routine after a time. As soon as one of the youngsters had had enough he let one of the others get to the entrance first. The smallest one continued to be thoroughly anti-social. If the three youngsters were sitting quietly, huddled together, and one of them suddenly began to gnaw at the itching quills of its sprouting feathers the little runt would lash out furiously at his bigger companions. It was often rather amusing to see one of the bigger youngsters humbly retreating before the little brawler's onslaught.

When they were seventeen days old the young were already sticking their necks out of the nesting hole, and were fed without the parents' having to bring their food inside the entrance. The adult birds only entered the hole to remove the droppings from the nest after they had fed their young. As was to be expected the parents brought food much more frequently than before and in larger amounts.

It was a good year for cockchafers. In the warm, dry spring weather swarms of them could be seen under the fruiting trees. So numerous were they that many branches had already been eaten bare, and I spent much time under the trees filming. While doing so I discovered another of the woodpeckers' hunting methods. In the course of previous observations I had seen them foraging for food round the trees, but now I saw that they had perfected a method of feeding on the wing. They scooped up cockchafers in their beaks in the same way as I had seen bee-eaters do in Crete. The woodpeckers did not find it easy to get at the thin, whippy branches favoured by the cockchafers. Instead they sat on the thicker branches and waited until a cockchafer flew into range. Immediately, one of the woodpeckers would dart towards its prey like a fly-catcher and in a flash pick it out of the air. The bird would then return to its perch on the oak branch and press the cockchafter into one of the notches it had carved in the branch. It then proceeded to dissect its prey, tearing off all the horny chitin from wing sheaths, head and thorax with practised movements of its beak. From morning till night the woodpeckers brought cockchafers for their young which were by now almost fully grown on this rich diet.

Five days after we had transferred them to their new home, one of the nineteen-day old youngsters made his first flight from the hole, an event which usually takes place between the twenty-first and twenty-third days. We were to blame for this premature first flight. As we had feared, the young birds had never really grown accustomed to the different living conditions in their new home. We had also had to remove the glass for cleaning more and more often as the youngsters began to clamber about the nest and dirty it. Although we covered our faces when we did this, the sight of our hands seemed to be enough to agitate the young birds considerably. It was on one of these occasions that a frightened young woodpecker made his premature first flight. It came to no harm, because the parent birds continued to look after it, but this made us stop filming. We had to leave Ludwigsburg, in any case, because Hummel had written to us that some green woodpecker young had just hatched out in an ideally suitable woodpecker hole in the Dülmen forest. After our experiences with the great spotted woodpeckers we were very keen to see what we could learn by observing other species.

By evening we had loaded our equipment and left, driving through the night, as we had often done before when time was pressing.

SEVEN

Infra-Red Photography with the Green Woodpeckers

In Dülmen the seasons change a fortnight or so later than at Ludwigsburg, so for the second time that year we enjoyed the blossoming chestnut trees, the golden yellow of the broom and the shimmering new green of the beeches, while the song of the thrush and the golden oriole sounded through the forest. While we had been away Hummel had kept an eye open for woodpeckers in his area and instructed his forestry workers to look out for occupied holes, but so far all efforts to track down the elusive green woodpeckers had failed.

As had so often happened before, chance played its part. One evening one of the forestry workers was bicycling home through a neighbouring part of the forest, when for some reason he dismounted and leaned his bicycle against one of the beech trees bordering the path. He had hardly done so when a green woodpecker darted out from behind the tree only a few inches from him. At the same time he distinctly heard a harsh, whirring sound. On walking towards it he found the entrance to a green woodpecker hole breast-high in the tree trunk. The young inside it were still very small, judging by their cries for food.

No sooner had we arrived when Hummel told the forestry worker to take us to the green woodpecker hole. So excited were we by the happy find that we had already covered part of the seven mile drive to the site before we realised that it was in a part of the forest under different ownership, and we should need a licence before we could start work. The position of the tree by the roadside also made things difficult. It might hinder our work considerably. We would not be able to conceal our activities; and it would be impossible to mount a twenty-four hour guard and explain what we were doing to passers-by. But our hopes rose when we left the smoothly surfaced main road and turned off on to the bumpy forest road. So secluded was the nesting site that we could safely disregard any possibility of being disturbed. Hummel had not exaggerated; it could not have been more suitable for our purpose. The nesting hole was only five feet off the ground, with a steeply inclined entrance, and behind it, where we would cut away the tree trunk and build the hide, there was a young pine plantation. Conditions were just right for building the hide at ground level.

It was important to find out where the nearest electricity supply was. From our many previous contacts with the green woodpeckers we knew that the methods we had used with the great spotted woodpeckers would have to be changed for these shy birds. While we were still mulling over our course of action by the hole we saw both woodpeckers arrive, but they did not dare approach us. Great spotted woodpeckers would have alighted impatiently near where we were standing, but the green woodpeckers remained under cover behind an avenue of trees fifty yards away, and watched us carefully until we walked off. We would have to use infra-red photography for them, and would need electric current to light their hole.

We found the owner of the forest on his estate near by. When we told him what we wanted to do, it turned out that he was an enthusiastic hunter and well remembered a full-length nature film of mine called 'The Song of the Preserve'. He immediately gave us permission to work in his forest and willingly sacrificed the green woodpecker tree. All he wanted from us was a promise that we would allow him to be present when we finally succeeded in getting a view of the green woodpeckers rearing their young.

As a further concession we were allowed to take the electric current we needed for our infra-red spotlights from the estate's supply. We paced out the distance to the hole. It was nearly a thousand yards; and I was afraid that the drop in voltage would be too big, but George had no doubts on this score. He said that it was possible to work out what the drop would be and use a thicker cable to offset it. I knew I could rely on his technical knowledge and experience, though it was not easy to obtain a thousand yards of cable in Dülmen. Also it was quite out of the question to lay the cable in the mornings and reel it up again every evening. We should have to take the risk of leaving it down for the whole period of our film work.

The tree seemed to be very rotten; its foliage was sparse and many branches at the top had withered and died. There was no need to saw it off at all, since it was light enough to be left alone. Working from the ground, we found it easy to open up the nesting hole. With a two-handed saw we cut away a wedge of wood four inches deep, laying open the back of the hole. All we needed to do then was to chisel away enough of the trunk to enable us to make our perpendicular saw cuts.

At Ludwigsburg we had discovered that the woodpeckers would not be unduly disturbed provided we replaced the part of their nest we had sawn away, so this time we installed the glass immediately and then covered it over. This saved us a day which was badly needed, because the nestlings' eyes were already open.

We had opened up the hole at eleven in the morning. I had arranged to stand by and see how the woodpeckers reacted to this, while George fixed the electric cable.

We had kept the parents away from the nest for an hour, so they should have returned in a few minutes with food for their young. Instead, a quarter of an hour went by before the hen finally dared to return. She was extremely cautious, flying from tree to tree in a gradual approach. At each stop she waited several minutes before going on to the next tree; finally she flew up to the hole. The spotted woodpeckers had also taken their time to enter the nest when they had noticed the pane of glass, but

77

their suspicion had been short lived. The green woodpecker was of quite a different temperament. She poked her head inside the hole a couple of times and then climbed round to the other side of the tree where she stayed for about ten minutes, quite indifferent to her young. I thought she was waiting for the male to arrive so that he could be the first to enter their changed dwelling, but then she climbed round to the entrance and disappeared inside it.

She stayed in the nest for three minutes and then appeared again and took up her position in a nearby beech. She stayed there for half an hour until the male announced his arrival with a melodious 'gleek-gleek-gleek-gleek'. After a long, cautious wait the male, still doubtful, entered the hole. He, too, spent three or four minutes feeding the young. All this strengthened my belief that there must be many differences in behaviour and habits between the green woodpeckers and the great spotted wood-peckers.

The woodpeckers fed their young, every forty to sixty minutes until sunset, and I used their long absences on foraging expeditions to make preparations for building the hide. This was easy, actually; for all I had to do was to 'plant' more trees among the pines already growing right up to the woodpecker tree. This would make the foliage so dense that the woodpeckers would not be able to see through it, so that all we would then have to do would be to build our hide among the trees.

George had managed to obtain more than a thousand yards of electric cable in the county town. We laid it by sunrise next day. We bridged the road near the farm with the cable and then laid it through a pine plantation, burying the valuable copper cable deeply enough for it to be hidden from any four-legged (and indeed, any doubtful two-legged) denizens of the forest. When we switched on in the afternoon the cable turned out to be too thin. Although it carried enough current for one spotlight, it was totally inadequate for four. It took us two more days to lay an additional four thousand yards of cable, a thousand yards for each lamp. We also completed our preparations for building the hide. We 'planted' so many

pine trees near the woodpecker tree that they looked like a natural plantation, and in no way disturbed the woodpeckers.

On the third day we made ready our building materials—wooden
poles, planks, canvas and branches for camouflage; and when the woodpeckers had flown off after the second feed we took two forestry workers as
reinforcements and went to the building site. The work had been planned
in such a way that everything would be finished when the woodpeckers
came back forty minutes later. The hide was built to enclose the cut-away
rear of the nesting hole, and darkened so that, when we uncovered the
glass, the woodpeckers would not realise that the hide was on the other
side. In the centre of the hide we erected a scaffolding and mounted the
infra-red lamps on it. When we had camouflaged the hide with branches
and leaves, we saw that the woodpeckers continued with their normal
activities as if nothing had happened.

We should have liked to begin filming immediately, but thought it
better to give the woodpeckers a bit more time to settle down, and decided
to make a start the following morning after the first feed.

At nine o'clock next morning our companions left us and we settled
down to wait for the return of the woodpeckers. We had already uncovered the glass and had again made sure that the hide was lightproof,
and that the woodpeckers could not see us or our equipment.

Half an hour went by before the first woodpecker flew up to the tree—
quickly, without uttering a call. The nestlings were some twelve days old.
Their tail and wing feathers were already growing, and their eyes had been
open for two days. They still huddled together in a pyramid for warmth,
but they could hardly hear the parent birds alighting at the entrance to
the hole, so loud and insistent were their cries for food. Their immature
bodies, long, skinny necks and broad beaks looked, in the dim light of the
nest, like the petals of some strange, quivering flower.

I wanted to find out what went on in the nest before we actually
started filming. Since the hide was completely dark, we were able to get
so close that our noses almost touched the glass. We watched the green

79

woodpeckers, which are about the size of jays, feeding their young a few inches away from us. One of them poked its head into the hole several times. The quick alternation of light and darkness aroused the youngsters and they broke into ear-piercing cries which only ceased when the male entered the nest.

The hole was nine inches across and eighteen inches deep, and despite the fact that the young were eleven days old and stretched out their long necks for food, the parent still had to clamber down some eight inches into the nesting hole to feed them. He did this in his normal climbing posture. When he slipped inside the entrance he turned round and slid into the nesting hole with his body held upright. We were not surprised that he entered the nesting hole this way, for he is not very well equipped for tree-dwelling. His beak is not so hard as that of a typical tree-dwelling woodpecker, and his feet with their shorter toes, are not so powerful.

We waited excitedly for the next feed, for we had been struck by the fact that this kept the green woodpecker in the nesting hole for a surprisingly long time. As soon as the parent bird arrived it shuttled its beak from side to side to regurgitate some food, and then rammed it down the gullet of the nearest youngster. The green woodpecker does not carry food in its beak. Its oesophagus widens out into a crop-like pouch which can accommodate a large quantity of food. Again and again the cock pushed food down a youngster's gullet, fifteen portions in all, so that some of the nestlings were fed several times. In this way the green woodpecker in one flight provides his young with the same amount of food for which the great spotted woodpecker has to make many flights.

When the young were satisfied they huddled together again with their necks round each other; but the parent bird still busied himself with them for a while. We could not see what he was doing because he was standing on the floor of the nest, straddling it and thus blocking the light. It was on occasions like this that our infra-red film shots came in useful.

80

The young black woodpeckers
thrust their way towards the
male parent bird with
greedy cries for food

When the parent birds
are away the youngsters
huddle together in
a pyramid, for warmth.
With their necks
wrapped round each
other the naked young
birds find this the best
way of keeping warm

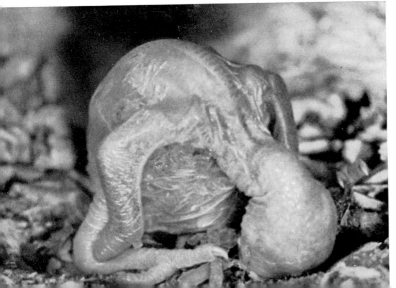

The youngster's thin
scrawny neck is still
too weak to support its
big, heavy head.
Being alone all the
nestling can do is rest
the weight of its head
on the floor
of the nesting hole

In infra-red photography (which we were using for the first time to film wild life), films can be made in complete darkness. Infra-red rays are trained on the subject and special infra-red film is used. Our 500-watt lamps were enclosed in metal boxes so that their rays were thrown forward through the infra-red gelatine filter. The resulting deep red glow was so dim that details in the hole could hardly be distinguished with the naked eye. From the moment the lamps were switched on it was apparent that they did not disturb the woodpeckers. They seemed to be ideal for revealing what was happening in the darkened nest, but in practice we soon found disadvantages. Infra-red film is so insensitive that we had to use four spotlights to light the nesting hole, and these had to be no further than four and a half feet away. Moreover, the spotlights could only be switched on for three minutes at a time or else the gelatine filters would begin to melt.

We wished our birds were fish, for tropical fish in aquaria will tolerate far greater heat than woodpeckers! The spotlights threw out so much heat that we could only switch them on for a minute at a time if we wanted to get a naturalistic record of events in the nest. The insensitivity of the film meant that we could only photograph well-lit subjects. A further disadvantage was that they had very little depth and appeared almost two-dimensional. Infra-red light was inadequate to record the abruptness of the woodpeckers' movements, so close-ups were out of the question. So we contented ourselves with general shots where the camera could take advantage of greater depth and record the whole scene.

As we were filming in a ready-made dark room we could make contact prints on the spot and check lighting and sharpness of detail. The first prints showed that the strength of the electric current varied with the amount of electrical apparatus in use at the farm, so we had to hang out our white distress signal more often than was pleasing to the woodpeckers. In the end the parents became so mistrustful that they stayed away up to two hours between feeds, having realised that something unusual was afoot in the dark fastness of their hole.

81

F

Because of the technical difficulties I have described, only some of the many shots we made during the next ten days were of any use, but they did reveal many hitherto unknown phenomena. We discovered that the parents clamber down into the nest after feeding in order to remove their brood's droppings, having first prodded the youngsters' hindquarters—the only way in which they can be made to excrete. In contrast to the great spotted woodpecker, the green woodpeckers do not carry off the droppings in their beaks, but swallow them on the spot.

During their parents' absences in the daytime the young began to make increasing use of their beaks and tongues. While they were still huddled on the floor of the nest the rotten sides of the hole proved an irresistible attraction. They spent more and more time hacking away playfully at the decayed wood with their short, soft beaks and stretching out their surprisingly long tongues, which in adult green woodpeckers are five times as long as their beaks. The green woodpecker can shoot out its tongue in any direction and so seek out the insects it feeds on, even when they are hidden in twisty crevices in the bark.

We followed the rearing of the young green woodpeckers until they were twenty-four days old and fully fledged. Since there were five of them in the restricted space of the nesting hole there was some squabbling, but it never assumed serious proportions. At this age they must often have been really hungry as they had to wait an unusually long time for the parent birds to return from their foraging expeditions. Even when they were competing with each other for food, however, they were not nearly so savage and vicious as the young great spotted woodpeckers.

After twenty-five days the young were fully fledged. The green woodpecker is the only one of our native species whose young have a different plumage from the adults until moulting time in spring. In contrast to the grey-green underside of the adult birds, the young have spots of deeper colour from breast to belly, and the red head stripe of the male is already bright and well-developed.

When the young had reached this age we ended our observations and filming of events inside the hole. The young were now fed from outside, and when they clustered at the entrance at feeding time they blocked out the light so that we could see hardly anything in the hole. Two yards away from the entrance we dug a trench, roofed it over with turf and used it to make further observations of what was happening with the woodpeckers. We had already noticed that young great spotted woodpeckers were fed much less frequently towards the end of their time in the nest. It was the same with the young green woodpeckers, they clamoured for food more loudly and more often, but the parent birds took little notice, often sitting idly for three hours on a neighbouring birch tree. Their urge to feed their brood diminished noticeably; and when they answered the unceasing clamour of the youngsters with their own call it was obviously to try and lure them out of the nest. However, the parents still defended the neighbourhood of the nest from intruders. Once an unknown green woodpecker landed near by. Our male immediately went for the stranger and drove him off. Twice we saw a great spotted wood-pecker fly up to the nest, attracted by the cries of the young. Both times, before we could see whether the stranger would feed the youngsters (something which has been observed many times among birds nesting in holes) the green woodpecker appeared and drove it off.

If we had correctly estimated the age of the young woodpeckers, they left their hole when they were twenty-seven days old. For some weeks after that their calls showed that the family was still together. The forest yields such a wealth of food in the spring that the young can fend for themselves from the first day they leave the nest, but the parent birds still provide food for them for a considerable time.

EIGHT

Inside the Black Woodpecker's Nest

When we showed our photographs of the great spotted woodpeckers and the green woodpeckers to a group of experts they were almost unanimous that we had enough material to make a nature film. Only one raised an objection—Professor Konrad Lorenz, whose researches into animal behaviour are well-known. He had been sceptical about our work, he said, but our photographs had convinced him that it was possible to film woodpeckers in their holes. It would be a pity if we did not exploit our opportunities to the full. We had not been able to film the young of the great spotted woodpecker before they were half grown, and we had succeeded in filming the green woodpeckers only when their eyes were already open. Now that we had the knowledge and experience we ought to make a film without any omissions, and this would increase the value of our previous work. Lorenz went on to say that he thought the best species to film was the black woodpecker since this bird moved more slowly and therefore his movements could be studied better in the film.

Such an undertaking would, we knew, require increased funds, but our Institute rallied to our support and the way was clear for our greatest adventure with the woodpeckers. For this tricky undertaking we enlisted the help of Jochen Scheven, a young ornithologist who was interested to observe how we would outwit the black woodpeckers in their holes.

We were very lucky in finding a hole only twenty-two feet up. Most of the nesting sites of this large woodpecker which I had so far found in the beech forest had been more than thirty feet off the ground. At that height it would have been almost impossible to finish building a hide in time for filming. The hole we had found now was in Hummel's territory, and this was a further piece of luck, because nobody else would have allowed us to touch the tree. It was a beech more than a hundred years old, and a perfect specimen, growing straight up almost thirty-six feet beyond the black woodpecker hole.

We were less happy when we made our way to the tree with Forester Hummel and looked at its wide canopy. We knew that felling the tree above the level of the hole was out of the question. On the other hand, branches at the top of the tree would catch the wind, and once we had opened up the hole, the tree would be in even greater danger than was the one at Ludwigsburg of being snapped in two by a strong wind. In answer to our cautious questions, Hummel said: 'When it's stormy don't climb the tree. It will hold all right in good weather'. He did not know that this time we were forced to work every day, whatever the weather, and we, therefore, decided to let the matter rest for the time being, because his permission to open up the nest was in itself a great concession.

Our plan was to build a hide in the tree and use the same working methods as we had with the green woodpeckers. The only difference was that this time, we should be eighteen feet above ground level.

Hummel supplied our timber by felling a large number of thirty-foot trees in a nearby pine plantation. We had kept a constant watch on the black woodpeckers so that we would know the second day of incubation. This was the best time to start building our hide, as the woodpeckers would by then have got into the routine of sitting on their eggs. If our earlier observations were anything to go by the young would take twelve days to hatch, so we would have ten days to build our hide.

In the afternoon of May 3rd we dragged the wooden uprights of our hide into position. We had worked out their length exactly so that we could bury the ends three feet deep in the ground. The floor of the hide

85

would be built at a height of fifteen feet, and from there the last nine feet of the uprights would form the supports for the sides of the hide and its roof. The hide would have to be much bigger, this time, to accommodate the extra infra red lamps and equipment we would be using. To save time we erected the uprights of the hide while the male was still sitting on the eggs. When the hen relieved him and he flew off, we kept her away from the nest long enough for us to secure the uprights to the tree with strong beams.

We had calculated that the hide would have to bear a weight of some five hundredweight, so we used five-inch nails to fasten the beams to the tree and to the uprights. Our hammering resounded through the forest, and the woodpecker disappeared among the beech trees uttering loud warning cries. Nevertheless, ten minutes after we had stopped work the hen reappeared flying low, and a few minutes after that she entered the nesting hole. So she was not put out by the changes our building had made! That was an encouraging sign. I remembered what Professor Lorenz had said—that the only way to find out whether the secretive black woodpecker was more difficult to film than other species was to try.

Next morning we finished the floor of the hide by laying planks across the beams. The platform was eight feet long, and we used weathered, dark-coloured planks so that they would not attract the woodpeckers' attention too strongly. Every time we broke off work we covered them with leafy branches. Standing on the platform, we started on the tree trunk with hammer and chisel. We would have preferred to use a two-handed saw—as we had with the green woodpeckers—but it would have been criminal folly on this mighty beech. Opening up the hole would be a very risky business. We had to keep the opening we were making small, in order not to weaken the tree.

We were afraid that our hammering might harm the eggs, so we removed them from the nest each time we went to work. Taking them out of the hole was quite easy as the entrance of the hole was wide enough to admit a man's arm easily. We put the eggs in a woollen pouch which we held next to our bodies for warmth. To divert the birds from the nesting hole while we were working, we imitated the sounds of tree felling, and every time the parents approached we walked about the forest hitting tree trunks with a cudgel.

We had noticed on the first day that the otherwise somewhat timid black woodpeckers were just as bold in flying to their nesting sites in the face of disturbances as were the great spotted woodpeckers.

Generally black woodpeckers relieve each other every seventy to ninety minutes during the incubation. We never worked on the tree trunk for more than half an hour at a time, and then left the birds in peace for three hours—because we thought it dangerous constantly to prevent them from relieving each other on the eggs. Each time we stopped we covered the spot where we were working on the tree with a piece of board the same colour as the bark, so that the birds would not notice that we were cutting into the rear of their nesting hole.

After we had chiselled into the tree trunk for five days, our admiration and respect for the black woodpeckers' abilities knew no bounds. They had completed their hole, twenty by ten inches in size, in twenty-three days. The hole we were making would have to be twenty-four inches by twelve and at least seven inches deep. The deeper we chiselled into the tree the more difficult it became, until we had to give up because half an hour's hard work achieved so little.

'If we carry on at this rate, we shan't even be finished in two weeks' George shouted down from the platform, wiping the sweat from his forehead.

Only a few minutes remained before we would have to camouflage our work again and give way to the insistent cries of the woodpeckers. We sat down on some pine logs, keeping an eye on our woodpecker hole from afar, and held a council of war. By the second day we had already begun to doubt whether we would be able to carry out our task with hammer and chisel, and we had made far-reaching enquiries as to what other tools and methods we might employ. Electric drills, power saws and power planers had all been condemned as unsuitable, no doubt because nobody had ever used power tools for this job before. We decided that our only hope, and that a slight one, was an electric drill which would penetrate at least two inches into the trunk. If we used a powerful motor we were bound to make quicker progress.

Power supply was a problem, just as it had been on our last filming expedition. There was a farm with electricity in the neighbourhood; but it was over a mile away, and after the troubles we had had in the past with fluctuations in voltage and power failures we did not want to risk it. We decided to acquire a generator and make our own power station. A friend of ours in Munster, Mr. Throner, made enquiries and informed us that a generator was available for hire in a little town sixty-five miles away. The generator weighed three hundredweight and took two days to transport over the soggy forest roads. We dragged it into position a hundred yards away from the woodpecker hole in a thickly wooded dip, and built a weatherproof roof over it.

The birds had been sitting on their eggs for ten days when we resumed our onslaught on the beech with an electric drill. It was not easy to manipulate—first because it weighed nearly five pounds, and second because the bit often jammed in the wood. Ten minutes went by before we had loosened a piece of wood big enough to make chiselling it out worth while. 'We shall need another four days for this job', said George. 'It is only two days till the eggs hatch', I replied, 'and we shall need another two days to finish the hide. We shan't make it at this rate. The only way is to try to work even when the woodpeckers are sitting on their eggs'.

We had already accustomed the birds to the building of the hide. Each time before leaving the site, we piled pine and fir branches on the platform; and the birds soon grew used to this change in their immediate surroundings, because all the trees around them were changing too, sprouting leaves and buds as May advanced.

To allow plenty of space for our cameras and other equipment, the hide was to be six feet high inside. To darken it we used tar-paper this time. It was cheaper than canvas and was also waterproof. We remembered how unpleasant it had been on one occasion during very bad weather, when the heavy rain had poured into the hide at such a rate that we had been unable to keep the cameras and lamps dry. The tripods had been inadequately insulated, so that every time we touched anything we got an electric shock.

This time we were not taking any chances and were determined that our hide would be thoroughly waterproof. To do this we needed more time than one half-hour shift every three hours. We had been working on the woodpeckers' hole for eleven days, and had also nailed up the horizontal supports for the walls of the hide. We wanted to complete our preparations in time to record the happenings in the nest from the very beginning: but as our methods were not fast enough we decided to carry on with making the side walls of the hide and nailing on the tar paper even when one of the birds was sitting on the eggs. We began by making the back wall, six feet from the hole, using very small nails. When the woodpecker remained in the hole, we became more daring; next day two of us hammered away at the roof and the sides. In the end we were working less than two feet away from where the woodpecker was sitting on the eggs.

When Forester Hummel paid us a visit and heard our hammering ringing through the forest he shook his head. 'Do you really think the woodpeckers will still co-operate if you actually nail wooden beams to their tree?', he asked. Soon, he was to see with his own eyes that the woodpeckers would still co-operate.

We worked on until loud cries of 'krri-krri-krri-krri' announced that one of the woodpeckers was returning to relieve its mate. This was the signal for us to cover up the hide and withdraw.

We kept a look-out from our vantage-point and told the forester not to take his eyes off the entrance to the woodpecker hole. Through binoculars we saw the approaching woodpecker male land as usual on a pine branch some four yards from his hole. With neck outstretched he glanced quickly over to the hole and then flew across to it, giving his loud jackdaw-like call of 'pee-ak' as he went. As the hen flew out of the hole, the male entered it without a moment's delay. Hummel smacked his knee with his hand and exclaimed: 'Gentlemen, if I were to tell anybody what I have just seen they would think it was another tall story!' His amazement renewed my fear of unexpected setbacks. The fact that there was a bird in the hole all the time we were working did not prove that it was sitting on the eggs. It could well have been clinging to the side of the nesting hole and have not gone near them. Success was by no means certain.

The next day, May 13th, my colleagues went to the woodpeckers without me. I stayed at the Max Planck Institute to try and film the mating of some newts. That Sunday was my lucky day. I had tried before, without success, to make such a film through the glass bottom of the aquarium. This time I had just managed to do so when George came in with the glad news that the young woodpeckers were beginning to hatch.

Ever since we had hired the generator one of us had always spent the night near the woodpeckers. We dared not leave the site unattended because everybody knew about our expedition and we could not run the risk of having our plans ruined by meddlers, even though we were working in a secluded part of the forest. We had prepared very comfortable, waterproof accommodation for our night watches, with plenty of room for one person to lie down. We had to be in position before first light because we wanted to film the way the woodpeckers shared their tasks, and to record any changes in the daily routine.

Scheven had been on watch that night, and soon after first light, at ten to five, had seen the male bird leave the hole with something white in his beak. Since some people hold the theory that woodpeckers do on occasion remove their brood to another hole, he assumed that what the male was carrying in his beak could only be an egg. This theory has never been proved wrong, so Scheven's assumption was more or less justified.

Five minutes later the male returned and stayed in the nesting hole until relieved by the hen at five o'clock. George arrived at six o'clock and when the sitting bird was relieved by its mate, decided to investigate. He placed a ladder against the tree and climbed up. As he reached the upper rungs he thought he heard young crying for food. Very gently he felt around inside the nesting hole with his fingertips. Two tiny woodpeckers had hatched out and two more eggs lay near them. What the woodpecker had had in his beak when Scheven saw him was an empty eggshell. At this point the woodpecker parents flew excitedly up to the tree; and George deemed it wiser to leave them alone for the rest of the day and let them hatch the remaining eggs.

The eggs had taken exactly twelve days to hatch out. Worried, I asked George how long it would be before we could start filming. He told me that the wall dividing us from the nesting hole was now so thin that we should certainly pierce it at our next attempt. At the same time we should be able to make the front of the hide fast to the tree.

George was right. At half-past seven the next morning we broke through into the nesting hole. There was no time to be lost. The glass had to be fitted without delay because the birds would have been more disturbed by a rough piece of wood there than by a smooth pane of glass.

When we had first started to use the electric drill the male woodpecker had reacted to its monotonous hum by vigorous drumming. Now his agitation was far greater because of the young, and he drummed fast and furiously overhead in the beech tree. The parent woodpeckers were so worked up by our presence that Scheven had great difficulty in keeping them at a distance; and they flew boldly up to us as if they were going to attack. After forty minutes the glass had been fixed in place and the hide made fast to the tree and blacked out. I had been keeping the four young warm and could now return them to the nest.

We had yet to instal the infra-red lamps, but decided to wait for four hours to give the parents time to feed their young. But now that the hide was finished I could not resist the temptation to climb up into it and

91

find out what could be seen. At last I was going to have the chance of visiting the fairy-tale birds of my childhood! The hide was in total darkness except for a glimmer of light showing through the glass from the nesting hole entrance, and it took some time before my eyes became accustomed to the dim twilight and I could see the sleeping youngsters.

I had never awaited the woodpeckers' return with such excitement, and only now did I realise that I was going to see something no human eye had ever seen before.

My companions had left and were about a hundred yards away when I heard a woodpecker's claws strike the tree. I was standing at the glass only a few inches from the entrance and hardly dared breathe when the big woodpecker poked his head into the nest for the first time. The black woodpecker's powerful beak, brightly rimmed piercing eyes and fiery nape-patch were visible for only a moment. Then he withdrew frightened. This happened twice more and I had the feeling that the woodpecker knew I was there. He seemed to look me straight in the eye. In reality of course it was only the glass that he found strange and he was assimilating the change before venturing into the nesting hole.

Several anxious minutes went by. Only later was I told that the woodpecker had flown to the next tree and from there had inspected his tree from every angle. Ten minutes later I again heard him climbing up the tree trunk to the entrance hole. This time he even gave his jackdaw-like call. The barriers were down.

When he had reached the entrance, he looked at the glass several times in a frightened manner and then entered the nest. As I had surmised that he would, this tree-living bird clambered about his deep nest with his head down. The scene was indescribably beautiful as the big bird worked slowly down the deep funnel of his nesting hole to feed his young. When he entered the nest he regurgitated some food into his beak and then began to rouse the nestlings who had heard neither his calls nor the noise of his entry. They were huddled together in a pyramid for warmth and did not respond to the gentle touch of the chisel-like beak on their backs, necks and wings. I could see (much more clearly than with the great spotted woodpecker) that the parent bird had to find the swellings at the side of the youngsters' beaks before they could be fed. But at the first touch they stretched out their necks and opened their beaks wide for food.

Though light conditions were normal in the nest I observed that the parent woodpecker still had to search for the right spot on each youngster's head. Then I noticed that the nestlings had several special markings which eased the parents' task of finding their hungry beaks and feeding them during the first few days when they were still blind. Their beaks were tipped with white and the ends of their tongues were brightly coloured, as I could see when they opened their beaks to be fed. These markings disappear when the young birds' eyes open.

Our male woodpecker roused each youngster in turn, and to my amazement his beak disappeared almost entirely down each youngster's skinny throat as he fed it. He had brought so much food that he fed each of the four youngsters three times, and still had some left over. The nestlings had had enough, however, and did not respond further to the offered food, so he swallowed it again.

Feeding had lasted three minutes, during the whole of which the parent bird had been hanging head down. He stayed in this position some time longer while he cleaned out the nest. He tapped each nesling's hindquarters with his beak to stimulate excretion. Then he straddled the young and covered them with his soft breast feathers to keep them warm. He remained in this position until relieved by his mate. Normally, black woodpeckers never leave their young unattended, as I was to see during my four-hour watch.

There was hardly enough room in the nest for the male to look after his brood. He had to keep his head and tail stretched upwards and put his legs with their fearfully sharp claws sideways. Every time he changed his position he took care not to catch any of the young with his claws. Most of the time while he was keeping his brood warm he kept his eyes closed, but no noise escaped his attention. As soon as he heard the call of

93

a thrush or some other small bird he was wide awake and climbed up the side of the nest to the entrance hole to see that all was well. Every now and then, he tapped each youngster with his beak to see whether it needed to excrete again and then resumed his vigil.

After eighty minutes I heard the hen making her call in the distance. The male also heard her, but stayed with the young till she had come quite close. We had already seen the way they changed over while still sitting on the eggs. Always the relieving bird took up a position on the trunk of a pine four yards away and started to call 'pee-ak, pee-ak', until its mate emerged from the hole. If there was no response to its call it flew up to the entrance and asked again to be let in. Once the male's call was ignored, and I saw him actually enter the hole. Only then did the hen yield her place. Now the hen was calling from the pine tree. The male's response was quite remarkable. The first 'pee-ak' had hardly died away when he began hammering furiously at the side of the nesting hole. It was the same hammering that I had heard so many times when the woodpeckers were making their holes. Just as the male had then invited the hen to relieve him with ceremonial movements of his beak, so now he invited her with the same rites to take over guarding the young.

This, for me, surprising discovery reminded me that I had once heard the same hammering, somewhat muffled by the bark of the tree, during hatching time, when I was filming woodpeckers from a ground level hide. At that time I had not realised what it might have meant. I thought then that the bird was completing the tunnelling of its nesting hole while guarding the eggs.

After several more calls from the hen the black woodpecker male yielded his place to her. When it was time for the hen to be relieved seventy minutes later, she in her turn hammered three or four times on the side of the nest before making room for the male. This time the hen was away for ninety minutes. When she returned there was a burst of hammering, seven strokes in all, followed by twelve more in rapid succession. After this I heard a soft, cooing sound for the first time.

Apparently this cooing call is a sign of heightened excitement among black woodpeckers.

At the very moment that the male left the hole I heard Scheven and George hurrying along to the hide. They had been concealed in the bushes nearby and rushed over so quickly that the hen was not able to get inside the hole. Everything was now ready for the infra-red lamps to be set up so that we could start filming. All the other equipment had been prepared, the cable laid from the generator to the hide and the battens for the lamp gallery sawn to length. Nevertheless, there was still some hammering to be done, and it took half an hour. Then at last we could get the lamps into their permanent position. After our experiences with the green woodpeckers we did not want to set them up and take them down every day. The hide was sturdily constructed and weatherproof, so everything could stay where we had put it. When filming was over for the day we could leave the hide just as it was and so reduce the risk of disturbing the woodpeckers to a minimum.

I wanted to use the next approach flight of the hen bird to make some test films, because the youngsters were growing so fast that we could not afford any more delay. We had installed five infra-red lamps six feet away from the hole with two movie cameras behind them. One camera had a wide-angle lens and would be used for filming the entire nesting hole interior; the other, with a more powerful lens, would be used for close-ups of the woodpeckers.

While George and I were making our preparations for a long stay we switched on the infra-red lamps, having first pushed aside the gelatine filters.

Scheven kept banging a stick against the surrounding trees, ensuring that the woodpecker did not return too soon. When we called out that we were ready he stopped and switched off the generator, because it was essential that there should be no noise while the hen was approaching the nesting hole.

She approached so softly that nobody heard her until her cry of 'pee-ak' told us that she had already reached the entrance to the hole. The next moment she had climbed down to the young. We had the whole afternoon to take photographs so we thought it better to leave the woodpecker alone after the noise that had been going on earlier. Instead we decided just to watch her tending the young. Both for George and me the next few minutes, while the woodpecker fed her young so close to us, were the most beautiful we had ever experienced in all our wild life work. 'My word', said George, 'if we succeed in making a sound film of the black woodpeckers in their nest, it will make a wonderful show for the International Ornithological Congress in June. We must do it somehow!'

A quarter of an hour went by. Inside the nest the hen woodpecker had fallen asleep in her usual position, straddled over the young to keep them warm. We gave Scheven (at his observation post near by) the signal to switch on the current, so that we could make our trial films. A few minutes later we heard the generator motor start up. The woodpecker did not stir. We had connected the lamps to a small switchboard in the hide, three to one switch and two to the second, and a built-in resistance in the circuit allowed the wattage to be increased gradually. When the five lamps were switched on, the sleeping woodpecker was bathed in a ghostly deep red radiance, but slumbered on oblivious of our presence and of the glass let into the rear of the nesting hole. Her plumage was slightly ruffled, her head sunk deep between her shoulders. When she opened her eyes it was not because of the lamps. What wakened her was the sound of a switch which we had been unable to muffle completely. The whirring of the cameras did not disturb her at all. Now our hope grew that at last we would be able to make our greatest dream come true and film the black woodpeckers in their nesting hole.

We stayed in the hide for five hours taking photographs from every angle and noting camera distances, apertures and light values ready for filming operations. With the lamps switched off the hide was so dark that we could have developed our films on the spot; but we decided that that it was safer to wait till we got back to our studio. So much heat was

The lesser spotted woodpecker, no bigger than a sparrow, also keeps its nest clean and carries droppings out of the hole in its beak

The youngsters, still blind, made no response when prodded in the back, wings or neck by their parents

The parents' beaks had to touch the large swellings at the corners of the youngsters' mouths before they responded by raising their heads, opening their beaks and accepting the food

The big woodpecker pushed the whole length of his beak down the youngsters' throats

Hammering inside the hole
was apparently intended to make more
bedding for the youngsters

Although nearly eighteen inches deep
and ten inches wide the nesting hole was
too narrow for the sitting black
woodpecker who had to hold its tail
and beak upright

In May the cries of the growing youngsters clamouring
for food came from their nesting holes

generated by the 500-watt lamps in the tightly closed hide that the developer and fixer had become too warm and we could not hope to obtain satisfactory prints.

When the first negatives were developed that night, we suffered a terrible disappointment. Apparently the contrast between the black birds and the light-coloured wood of the hole was too great for the infra-red film to register accurately. Our trial shots showed either properly lit birds against a dazzling background or a clearly visible nesting hole with vague black shapes in it. Understandably enough, we were greatly discouraged, but George remained confident in the face of all doubts. 'The lamps are too close to the hole', he said, 'and they are too strong. What we have to do is reduce the lighting and develop the negatives more slowly'.

The next morning, therefore, we rebuilt the lamp scaffolding and then rearranged the lamps, using a photometer to get the distances correct. The next batch of negatives turned out rather better and we decided that they could be used as scientific evidence of our observations. Nevertheless, it was clear that a great deal of detail had been lost because of the lighting conditions. In the past we had always considered that conditions during the making of a film should not have to be forgiven by the audience, who were entitled to the best that skill and know-how could produce. We therefore knew that we would never be completely satisfied with what we had done so far.

While filming the green woodpeckers, we had been helped by the fact that their holes had dark-coloured, weathered walls which did not offer much contrast to the birds' grey-green plumage. We had already considered darkening the sides of the black woodpeckers' nesting hole, which they would surely not have resented, but did not do so because there was no guarantee that it would achieve the desired result. Instead I decided to try and get the black woodpeckers used to normal spotlights. My companions shook their heads doubtfully when I told them of my plan, but on the afternoon of May 16th, when the young woodpeckers were four days old, we made the attempt. From three o'clock onwards I sat in the hide with George. No special precautions were necessary. All we had to do now was to raise one of the infra-red lamp filters a quarter of an inch so that a narrow beam of light would shine into the nesting hole when the lamp was switched on.

We decided to begin operations after the woodpecker had entered the hole and begun feeding the young. The hen arrived first, but we knew that her nesting urge was not as strong as the male's, so we did not have the courage to switch on the lamp. Later we realised our mistake. Another eighty minutes went by before the male flew up to relieve his mate. When he had started feeding the nestlings and was pushing food down the second youngster's gullet I cautiously switched on the lamp with shaking hands. The panic-stricken woodpecker opened his wings and fled from the hole. He could not have been more scared if someone had let off a gun near him, and, although we had fixed the glass very firmly in position, it rattled so loudly when the woodpecker fled that I thought that he had shattered it.

Scheven had been watching the hole through binoculars and he told us afterwards that the black woodpecker had flown away in such agitation that it was doubtful whether he would ever return to the young. I still remained confident, however. The woodpecker had not been frightened off by the presence of human beings, so could not connect us with what had happened.

I expected the parent birds to return to the nesting site together as they often did when there was a threat of danger, but after half an hour the male woodpecker returned alone. He alighted on a pine tree fifty yards from his hole and began slowly preening himself. Again and again he drew his beak through his tail and wing feathers or pecked at his breast and back feathers. He continued in this way for ten minutes. It was obviously the expression of an inner conflict—a 'displacement activity' such as often arises in animals when two opposing drives battle against each other. On the one hand the woodpecker wanted to return to his young, left unprotected for so long, and on the other hand the fright he had just had held him back.

We lay behind the bushes, waiting impatiently for his decision. We sincerely hoped that the woodpecker would finally return to his hole and take the young under his warm wing. If he did not we should be grievously disappointed. Several times he made as if to fly off, but each time stopped at the last moment and began preening himself again. Just when we thought that he had at last decided to return to the nest he flew off out of sight with excited cries.

We were relieved that Hummel had not witnessed this distressing scene. If he had been with us he would have made the prospect of the woodpecker's return seem even more remote, and would have expressed grave doubt as to whether we should ever succeed in filming them. After another quarter of an hour the male woodpecker suddenly reappeared, perched on the pine tree and stared straight at the entrance to the hole. Then he softly took up his call of 'pee-ak' and our hopes rose. They rose still higher when he flew towards his hole, but before he reached it he shied away in terror. His flight was so erratic and uneven that we thought he might have been frightened off by some new danger. This was not the case, however. He was still affected by the fright he had had when the lamp had been switched on earlier. Now we were sure that he would not enter the nesting hole again at least for the time being.

An hour and a half later we heard the hen approach. Her mate had long since flown away, and we were very pleased about this, because there would not be any distraction while she flew up to the hole. Although the youngsters had been left unattended for over an hour, we hoped that they had not come to any harm, because the sun was quite hot. Still, it was high time they were fed.

The hen did not seem in the least surprised that her calls had not been answered and that the male was not in the nest. She climbed inside to feed the young.

The day was drawing to its end now and in the normal course of things, the male would return in an hour and a half, feed the young for the last time, and then stay with them overnight. We attached particular importance to this last changeover because we knew that the hen would leave as soon as her time was up and spend the night in another hole of her own. We waited tensely to see whether the male would return and keep guard over his brood.

At eight-thirty exactly, when the sun was sinking behind the beech trees, the male came back. He alighted on the pine tree opposite the hole as if nothing untoward had happened and called to the hen, ready for the changeover.

'After such a long absence', I said, 'his urge to return to the nest is strengthened. Apart from that he is used to spending the night there. This time he will go inside'. My jubilation was premature, for what happened next was one of the most critical events we had ever had to contend with in our work with animals.

When she heard her mate's call the hen quietly left the nest, which meant that everything was in order. Ten minutes later the male had still not moved from his perch, and when he did fly up to the hole he shied away again as he had done before. His urge to enter the nest was evidently not strong enough to counter the memory of what had happened that afternoon. He started flying backwards and forwards in front of the nest, hovering in his flight now and again and looking inside the hole for some seconds. But he did not dare alight.

We were watching from under cover. All round us the forest breathed an atmosphere of peace. Tree frogs and toads were already croaking their nuptial calls in the soft twilight. The night-jars were churring in the pine grove and the mistle thrushes were chanting their usual evening song.

As night began to fall we realised that the young woodpeckers would die if the male did not enter the nest and keep them warm overnight. If we had made our experiment with the hen, we would not have had anything to worry about and the male would now have been on guard. If he did not enter the nest now, we should have to resort to keeping the young warm ourselves. It was the only way. From previous observations we knew that the hen would arrive to feed the youngsters at five in the

100

morning, so we could put them back shortly before that. The hen would probably continue to rear them singlehanded, though there was a good chance that the male might resume his normal activities the next day.

A few minutes later, when dusk was falling fast, the male woodpecker landed at the entrance for the first time and looked deep inside. Then he flew off, but returned immediately for a second inspection. The third time he went inside the hole for a little while. The fourth time he went inside the hole and then turned round and peered out.

'I don't trust him', said George. 'He is so agitated that he is likely to fly off unobserved, and then all is lost. From the way he is behaving now, I am sure that he will co-operate in the morning, but in the meantime we ought to take the young under our protection'.

By now there was so little light that we could no longer see clearly what was happening at the woodpecker hole, so I crawled to within ten yards of it under cover of the bushes, while George kept the area under observation. When I was close enough I peered through the bushes and saw the woodpecker have a final look round and then vanish into the hole. We stayed on watch half an hour longer until darkness had fallen and we could be certain that the woodpecker was asleep in his usual position, straddling his young.

That night we all camped out in the forest. In the first place our hut (where we took it in turns to sleep) could not accommodate so many guests, and secondly the night was warm enough to sleep out on a bed of pine and fir branches. The fragrance of pine resin and moss, the croaking of the frogs, the twinkling of the stars in the sky, the knowledge that the black woodpecker had returned to his young—all this would ensure a restful night. However, we still had to solve the problem of how to film events inside the nesting hole.

The sun was already drying the dew when we awoke, but it was not too late to see the first changeover in the nest.

The hen arrived at six-thirty, alighting straightaway on the lip of the entrance hole. Then she bent her body sideways to let the male woodpecker out. Secure in the knowledge that he had stayed all night with the young, we drove off happily to breakfast.

The hen could be expected to return for the second time in about three hours and we should then find out whether it would be possible to shoot our films or not. After the unsatisfactory results of our infra-red photography and the fright the spotlight had given the male woodpecker, my suggestion that we should make another attempt, this time with the hen, must have sounded pretty audacious. But my hopes were founded on the hunch that she might react differently, because there was no reason to suppose that both birds would react identically to the same situation.

We had made our first attempt when the woodpecker was fully occupied in feeding the young, but there were two other methods we had not yet tried. The first was to switch on the spotlights before the bird looked into the hole. If the woodpecker had been flying through the forest in bright sunshine it would perhaps not be put off by finding the nest quite well lit and might still feed the young. This method had the advantage of giving the woodpecker a chance to withdraw before entering the nest instead of running the risk of frightening it once it had done so. The other method we could use was to shine the lamps into the hole after the bird had straddled the youngsters and fallen asleep. I thought the second method was more likely to succeed.

When the third changeover took place at ten-thirty, we prevented the hen from entering the hole. George and I then dashed into the hide and trained one of the lamps through the glass at the back of the nest. The next moment the woodpecker alighted on the neighbouring pine tree and carefully took up a position from which it could see inside its brightly lit dwelling. Although we waited for half an hour the bird did not go in to its young. We switched off the lamp, and ten minutes later the hen appeared in the nest and started to feed the young as if nothing had happened.

Feeding had been over for half an hour and the hen was astride her brood, fast asleep. We switched on the first lamp and in a flash she was awake, her frightened eyes darting towards the light. Then, without

102

changing her position, she closed her eyes again and went to sleep. We immediately switched off the lamp and gave the bird ten minutes to come to terms with the situation. Then we switched it on again. The hen did not move. We had exactly half an hour left before the male was due to return. George pulled out the filter from the projector so far that at least half the light of the 500-watt lamp shone straight into the nest. At first we kept it on for only a few seconds, but then we removed the filter completely and kept the lamp switched on for a longer period. But even then the black woodpecker remained in her relaxed position straddling her young. After the panic of the day before this was a hopeful sign.

When the male announced his arrival ten minutes later and then appeared in the nest in front of us we did not dare move, and for the rest of the time that he was there we took special care not to disturb him. When he was relieved by the hen towards midday we proceeded with our experiment, increasing the amount of light until we had three spotlights going—a total of fifteen hundred watts. When the hen was again on guard in the nest later that afternoon, we switched on all the lamps, and in their 2500-watt beams we shot our first scene, the hen woodpecker straddling her young in characteristic posture.

The next day, May 18th, by using the same methods we succeeded in getting the male woodpecker accustomed to the spotlights, and we also managed to film the first scenes of the young being fed by the hen. We had now recorded on film at least the first complete phase of the rearing of their young by the black woodpeckers; and this made an interesting contrast with the film we had made of the great spotted woodpeckers and the green woodpeckers.

We had achieved what we had set out to do with the black wood-peckers. They had allowed us to shine spotlights on them in their nesting hole and film everything that went on. Now we could be their invisible (and uninvited) guests from morning till night, and film all that they did. Every plan had been fulfilled down to the last detail (or so we thought, at any rate), and nothing now stood between us and a complete film record

103

of the life of the young woodpeckers up to the time they left the nest. We continued to stand guard over our part of the forest. We had thoroughly waterproofed the hide so that the spotlights would be completely protected against the heaviest downpour. We thought the woodpeckers would be completely protected against rain, too. Their nest was deep inside the tree trunk and the entrance hole sloped upwards slightly. At the back was the tar-paper of the hide, securely fastened to the tree trunk with flat-headed nails, so there was no danger there either.

The rain came after a long drought. It started with a thunderstorm, and then became a country-wide downpour. We tried to curb our impatience. Filming was impossible because the wet weather prevented us from keeping the glass clean on the outside; and the glass was always misted over on the inside by the woodpeckers' breath. The woodpeckers were also having difficulty in finding enough food, and we thought it better not to disturb them. The rain was most unpleasant for the man on watch, because he had to spend his time in the small look-out trench in the sodden, dripping forest. It was as well we kept watch, however; for we were able to avert a catastrophe.

On the day after the thunderstorm we noticed that there was something amiss with the woodpeckers. Up to then one of them had always stayed with the young, but now both would fly away from the nest at irregular intervals. We attributed this behaviour to the difficulties of finding enough food. Perhaps the youngsters were hungry and their constant clamouring for food was making the parent birds fly off more frequently in search of it. We thought it best to check up and see that all was in order.

The next time the hen left the nest, George and I climbed up into the hide. Scheven kept the generator running to give us light. What an agonising sight greeted our eyes! The seven-day old, naked young woodpeckers were lying unprotected in the soaking wet nest. Rainwater was running into it round the sides of the glass. The tar paper had sagged so much in one particular place between two nails that a pool of water had

With its melodious cry of 'krrri-krrri-krrri-krrri' the black woodpecker hurries to its young

The young opened their eyes when twelve days old. They already weighed six ounces

The woodpecker holes were spotlessly clean. Here the woodpecker straddles a youngster while prodding its rump . . .

. . . in this way the youngster is made to excrete

they grew larger the young woodpeckers tried out their tongues and beaks more and more energetically

My wish had come true. I had found an 'open sesame' to the woodpeckers; and I could now film them using four thousand-watt spotlights

The young green
woodpeckers are
distinguished from
their parents
by their paler
colour and spotted
undersides

In order to record
behaviour that
we could not film
in the forest
we adopted some
young wood-
peckers. Even the
highly-strung and
anti-social green
woodpeckers
became my friends

collected there and was dripping down into the nest. Every two seconds a heavy drop fell on to the edge of the glass and water trickled down into the nesting hole, thoroughly drenching the wood waste and wood chippings lining its floor.

That was why the parent birds had become so restless. The youngsters were still lively; but something had to be done quickly, because unfledged young birds can contract pneumonia very quickly. George nailed a strip of tar-paper to the tree so that it formed a sub-roof and diverted the rainwater from the back of the nest. I took the youngsters out of the wet, dried them, laid them on a woollen scarf, and shone a spotlight on them. Finally, we took the wood chips out of the nest, wrapped them in a towel and pressed out the water. Then we spread them out on a spotlight to dry. It took an hour to dry everything out, and then we relined the floor of the nest with the wood chips and put the warm youngsters back.

Next day the sky was still obscured by heavy cloud and the forest steamed in the damp air but the rain had stopped and the life of the forest returned to normal.

Towards mid-day we were able to observe some amazing carpentry going on in the nest. The hen bird had been asleep for ten minutes after feeding the young, when she suddenly roused herself, climbed up the side of the nest and began to hammer away at it with her beak. Although the bird was not exerting herself to the full, this was no relief signal. She climbed up to a decayed spot on the wall which seemed to be softer than the surrounding wood, and hammered away for five minutes, apparently in the hope of pecking out some chips of wood. The spotlights were on; and with their help we could see everything much more clearly than when the woodpeckers had been carving out their holes in early spring. We used both cameras to make some film shots, and these bore out what we had already surmised—that the woodpecker almost always hammers with its beak slightly open, finding it easier this way to break off bits of wood from the tree.

This sudden reawakening of the urge to build could be explained by the woodpeckers' desire to reinforce the layer of wood chips and waste on the floor of the nest. When we had dried it, a proportion had been lost; and we had tried to make good the loss with file and chisel. Our efforts appeared to have been inadequate. In general, woodpeckers do not provide nesting materials other than the chips and wood waste which fall from the walls of the hole while they are hollowing it. But it seems that in an emergency they will make additional bedding for their young by resuming their work.

During the first eight days, while the youngsters' eyes were still closed, we noticed changes taking place in the feeding routine. Until they were two days old the youngsters opened their beaks only when the parent birds tapped the swellings on the sides of their heads. Taps or prods on other parts of their bodies produced no results. From the third day, whenever a youngster was fed, and consequently swung its head and stretched its neck out, these movements more and more communicated themselves to the others. After the fourth or fifth day the parents needed only to offer the youngsters food for them to open their beaks. Thus, during these few days, the young woodpeckers had learned that if one of them stretched out from their pyramid, it meant that food had arrived. The young also learned to tell when the parents had brought food, by the soft snoring sound made by the fortunate youngster which was having food crammed down its gullet. Just how strong an effect this 'snoring' had we were to see, later, with the green woodpeckers.

The young woodpeckers' eyes opened on the twelfth day. They already weighed six and a half ounces, and their egg teeth and beak swellings had all but disappeared. The young birds now took up their feeding positions the moment they heard the parent birds approach the entrance hole. At twelve days their upper and lower mandibles had already grown to a length of one and a quarter inches. No sooner had the young woodpeckers' eyes opened than they began trying out their beaks and tongues. We wondered how long the black woodpeckers would continue to keep their young warm.

106

Great spotted woodpecker parents do not stay in the nest for very long or visit it very often; and we had never seen the green woodpeckers stay long with their young, even while they were still unfledged. In contrast to this, our black woodpeckers stayed in the nest after feeding their brood, but this changed after the fifteenth day when the young birds were already so big and strong that they often jostled the parents. They found their enforced stay on the floor of the nest irksome, wanting to try out their beaks and their tongues on the sides of the hole. After eighteen days they began climbing about, and when they were twenty days old they took their food at the entrance.

During the many weeks we spent with the black woodpeckers we often heard passing hikers trying to guess the purpose of our hide. Most of them took it for a hunting cabin of some kind, and made off quickly when one of us cleared his throat, thinking that one of the foresters was inside. Others thought that our hide was something to do with army manoeuvres; we could usually get rid of these as well! During the final phase of our observations, we certainly posed a riddle for a family who happend to pass by. The path they had chosen lay within ten yards of our hide. Perhaps they would not have stopped but, not having heard them approach, we happened to switch on the spotlights just at that moment. One of the young woodpeckers looked out of the hole at the excited group, and it must have been a strange experience for them to meet a black woodpecker who lived in a hole with electric light. It so happened that I had lit a cigarette a few moments before this and smoke, brightly illuminated by the spotlights, was pouring from the hole as if from a chimney. (When the youngsters were fully fledged, their greasy plumage used to rub against the glass as they ran about the nest, so we removed the glass when the parent birds were not there.) The hikers must have had many lengthy discussions about what was going on in the hole.

From the time the young hatched until they were twenty days old, the parent birds took turns in bringing food eight to twelve times a day. They fed their young, therefore, every ninety minutes on an average. The first foraging flight was usually made shortly before six o'clock in the morning, two hours after sunrise. The male had to wait in the nesting hole after his tour of night duty until the rising sun gave the hen the chance of finding enough food. The young were fed for the last time at sunset at about eight o'clock.

Feeding became more frequent when the fledglings were twenty days old. They were almost fully grown, and their food requirements had increased as a result. Shortly before the young left their nest on the twenty-fifth day, the parent birds slackened off noticeably in feeding their brood. On the twenty-sixth day the parents sat for hours on a branch in front of their hole and uttered their loud 'klee-ae' cry surprisingly often. In the course of that afternoon we observed only one feeding and the fledglings became so hungry that they craned far out of the entrance hole clamouring for food. The green woodpeckers had behaved in the same way. The parents stopped feeding their young altogether, and with excited cries tried to coax the youngsters out of the hole. On June 8th, when they were twenty-seven days old, the fledglings dared the leap from the hole.

None of them returned. This does not mean to say that they were glad to get away from a site which they had been forced to share with us for three weeks. In all my observations I have never found that young woodpeckers return to their original nest once they have left it. They spend the first nights in the open and then seek out a suitable new hole for themselves.

NINE

We Adopt Some Young Woodpeckers

With the departure of the young from their nest, we had finished filming all the important events in the woodpeckers' breeding cycle. Woodpeckers do their drumming, bore their nesting holes, breed, and rear their young in the same place; and this attachment to one spot had proved very useful to us. Now they were on their own, free to roam the forest and settle where they liked and where they could find enough food. It would have been a waste of time to build a hide and hope that they would choose a branch immediately in front of the camera for their foraging or building operations. It would have been just as pointless to try to film from a hide the way they use their tongues as harpoons to spear beetle larvae, or as lime-twigs to snare ants from their anthills.

Nevertheless, we wanted to film all these things, and since they could not be done with wild woodpeckers we should have to try with captive birds. Those who have seen my film, and now read this, may think to themselves that the shots of woodpeckers using their tongues were staged by using 'trained' birds. But I should like to inform them that training usually means teaching an animal to do something it does not do in its natural state. Shots can only be called 'staged' if they are of stuffed animals or tame ones in unnatural groupings or poses.

Our first concern was to capture some woodpeckers and keep them in conditions where they could behave perfectly naturally. The best method of doing this was to rear some birds ourselves, first finding a brood too young to be able to recognise their parents. Our plan was to house them, once fully fledged, in a roomy aviary which would approximate their natural habitat. Since we would be taking the place of the parent birds, we hoped that the young woodpeckers would behave in our presence as their instincts dictated, without the slightest fear.

We began work with three six-day old great spotted woodpeckers, housing them in a wooden nesting-box about the size of a shoe box, which we had made specially for the purpose. The bottom was covered with shavings and wood chips, and we had put rough bark on the sides ready for the day when the youngsters would try out their climbing abilities. After all our observations in the field we had no difficulty in imitating the feeding methods of the parent woodpeckers, using a short pair of tweezers. Whenever we tapped on the swellings at the sides of their beaks, the young birds at once held their heads up and took the offered food. Then, with another pair of tweezers we prodded their hindquarters and removed the droppings to keep the nesting box clean.

We had set up our headquarters at Buldern because we were already doing some filming there at the Max Planck Institute of Comparative Physiology, recording the growth and development of the polecat. We built our aviary at the Institute because we wanted to have the youngsters close by. They were already demanding their first feed at five in the morning, and had to be fed right through the day until after sunset. Obviously we hoped to be able to rear strong, healthy birds, and the best way to do this was to try and feed them as frequently as would have been the case in their natural state, that is to say, every two or three minutes. We would feed them every five minutes. As we were also working with the polecats we could not spend our time cramming food down the woodpeckers' throats, so this task fell to my wife. She thus spent most of the day with them; but George and I also still spent some time with them so that they would recognise us when the time came to start filming in the aviary.

We fed the young woodpeckers on a mash which we supplemented with egg yolk, grated hazel nuts and fresh ant pupae. As a treat we gave them mealworms. They flourished on this diet.

Their nesting box was completely enclosed except for a narrow slit in the top, but the front could be removed at feeding time. The young woodpeckers soon learned that the removal of the front of the box and the increased light that resulted were connected with feeding. As we approached we made clicking noises with our tongues to warn them that we were going to open the box and they soon grew to recognise this. I also considered it important for our future work to get them used to the sound from a very early age, so that contact would be maintained as they grew older.

Our great spotted woodpecker brood was ten days old when fierce disputes began to break out. This time it was the smallest of the three youngsters which had to bear the brunt of the pecking that went on. It was very retarded in its growth, even though we had given it extra food and attention. In its natural state it would have been fed by its parents only when its stronger brothers and sisters had eaten their fill. With a mealworm held in a pair of pincers we would lure the stronger youngsters to one side while we tried to give the weakling some extra food. As it took the food with a typical snoring sound the others would hear it, clamber over and hammer savagely at the little runt with their beaks. In the end we had to remove the weakling from the box and rear it separately. There was no difficulty about this, as the young birds already had their feathers and no longer needed to huddle together to keep warm. On its own the weakling made rapid progress and grew into a particularly fine specimen. We did not know then that he would become especially attached to us because of the extra attention we had given him.

We started rearing three black woodpeckers when they were eighteen days old. After two days they freely accepted food from a pair of tweezers, and we no longer had to cram it down their throats. At twenty-five days they were quite tame. Every half-hour we took them out of their box and perched them on our hands while we fed them. After feeding they would climb up our arms to our shoulders, and put their long tongues in our ears. This was not really surprising because fissures and orifices always attract woodpeckers, however young. Putting their tongues in our ears had a special appeal for them, though not of course for us. If we tried to stop them, they would climb up on to our heads and carry on their search for food there, which was not as uncomfortable for us, as when they put their tongues in our ears! Our black woodpeckers did not content themselves with this, but insisted on finding out whether there was anything to eat under our scalps. After one of the youngsters had tried out its beak on my head, however, I never allowed any of them to climb on to my head again.

We fed our black woodpeckers on mash, mixing red ants and their pupae and hard-boiled egg yolk with it. They thrived on this diet and we could not have wished to see them making better progress.

When they were twenty-eight days old, my wife said: 'Your observations of drumming are incorrect. Black woodpeckers do not drum with their beaks at all. They use their tongues'. Later that day I heard drumming coming from the nesting box, and its rhythm was surprisingly like the drumming I had heard at breeding time. The woodpecker did not pause when I lifted off the front of the box. He was sitting half-way up the back wall, his tongue flashing back and forth against a corner of the box where he had already worn away the wood by hammering with his beak. This 'tonguing' of the box was certainly not the same as the sound we had heard so often coming from inside nesting holes. All the youngster was doing was trying out the tactile and prehensile qualities of its tongue. It was an amazing thing to see the force and rhythm with which his tongue struck the wood of the box, and to hear the noise it made.

Rearing the black woodpeckers and the great spotted woodpeckers presented no problems, but for a long time it looked as if we should fail with the green woodpeckers. I already knew from the published literature that it would be extraordinarily difficult to rear them, and that prospects of success were remote. When they are fully grown, green woodpeckers

The young woodpeckers' tails and
beaks do not reach their
full length until some months after
they have left the nest

After leaving the nest the black
woodpeckers hunt for ants, which
they mostly find
in rotten tree stumps

This black woodpecker has found
a beetle larva gallery.
With his supporting tail pressed
against the tree and his
climbing-iron claws clamped
onto the trunk, he can bring his
chisel beak into action
with great strength

Outside the breeding season
woodpeckers are out-and-out
individualists. Although a brood will
stay together with their parents
for some weeks after leaving
the nest, contact between them
grows steadily weaker

Hazel nut in beak, the great spotted
woodpecker was looking
for a suitable place to crack
open the shell

He could not find a crevice
wide enough, so he held the nut
with his breast feathers and
proceeded to hollow
out a recess in the wood

After several vain attempts
to crack the nut he again held it fast
and continued with his chiselling

He finally succeeded in making an
anvil and at once cracked open
the nut and ate the tasty kernel

The green wood-
pecker's sticky
tongue when fully
extended is five
times as long as
its beak

An ants' nest, with
the galleries cut
away and the
pupal chambers
fully occupied, was
placed against the
glass front of the
aviary, enabling us
to see, close up,
how the green
woodpecker used
his tongue

are so temperamental and anti-social that it is almost impossible to keep them in an aviary. Just how difficult it is to rear green woodpeckers is clearly demonstrated by the fact that Professor Heinroth, who has reared practically every European bird from the egg stage managed to keep only one green woodpecker until the first moulting time. We had, therefore, to work on the assumption that green woodpeckers would only submit to being reared by a human being until they were fully fledged and could fend for themselves.

The first green woodpecker we tried our luck with was twenty days old and was one of the brood from the hole which we had filmed. As we had frequently touched him while cleaning the glass let into the hole, I hoped that he would already have grown a little used to us. After we had taken him we left the strong and vigorous youngster to his own devices for a few hours, expecting him to start clamouring for food. He was almost fully grown and the swellings near his beak had almost disappeared. Even though we pressed against these with our tweezers he did not respond and we had to cram food down his throat, just as we had had to do before with so many other birds in similar circumstances. I took the woodpecker on my lap, opened his beak, put some food inside it with my tweezers, and then massaged the underside of his neck to make him swallow. In most cases this has the effect of stimulating a young bird's appetite and it will accept food freely. Our green woodpecker utterly refused to do anything of the kind, and tried his hardest to vomit out what was already in his beak. We could not continue in this fashion and had no choice but to take him back to the forest and release him.

As with our great spotted woodpecker we made our next attempt with two unfledged youngsters whose eyes were still unopened. They accepted food from tweezers without any difficulties. We fed them every half hour with ants, fresh pupae, mealworms and egg yolk mixed with a little mash. When we had been making observations in the forest, we had noticed that the parent birds often brought ants and pupae in their beaks, so they must have been an important part of their natural diet.

113

H

When the young green woodpeckers opened their eyes and continued to accept food from us, we thought we had reached our objective. Nevertheless, as their feathers began to sprout they grew weaker and weaker for no apparent reason, and their appetite flagged. We did not know what to do next. We had given them all possible care. We had kept them warm with heating pads and had laid wet cloths on the sides of the box to simulate conditions inside the nesting hole where the air is damp, thus preventing their tender rosy skins from becoming dry. Despite their natural diet, however, something seemed to be lacking.

'Perhaps what's missing is the saliva which the parent birds mix with the food before feeding their young', said my wife. We did not know, and finally concluded that the only thing to do was to put the green woodpeckers back in their hole and let their parents rear them. We had second thoughts, however, because we believed that if we put them back we would lose the contact we had begun to establish with them when their eyes opened. Therefore we put back only the weaker youngster.

On the way back, the notion came into my head of visiting a woodpecker hole we had been keeping in reserve. To our amazement the young were so well developed that they would be leaving the nest in two or three days' time. Still, we decided to try rehousing these strong youngsters too, and took four of them away with us.

As might have been expected they turned out to be as anti-social as the first lot. They stubbornly rejected every attempt to feed them and vomited the food out of their gullets. They started to lose weight; and all our efforts would have been doomed to failure, had we not tried a ruse I had thought of. I remembered the strong effect the sound of a feeding youngster had on the rest of the brood, so I put our little barely-fledged green woodpecker in the box with the four big ones. He still accepted food from us but it already looked as if we should soon have to return him as well to the care of his parents. In any case, it was worth trying to see whether we could influence the other four woodpeckers by feeding the small one. As a precautionary measure we had put the nesting box with the

114

youngsters in it into a dark basement room so that they would be less frightened by our presence there when the box was opened.

When I had fed the little woodpecker several times I touched the sides of the other birds' beaks with my tweezers and one of them snapped open his beak and swallowed several helpings of fresh ant pupae. The sound of his feeding had the desired effect on the remaining three youngsters and soon they were all freely accepting food from the tweezers. The barriers were down! The little one had saved the day, and we rewarded him by taking him back to his home in the forest.

We proceeded very carefully to the next stage of accustoming the green woodpeckers to us. First we made the light in the basement room stronger. Then we replaced the wooden front of the nesting box with glass so that the birds would become used to us. When they had grown enough to be able to leave the nesting box, we still kept them there together for a few days to strengthen the contact we had begun to establish between them and ourselves.

We had completed the aviaries while the youngsters were growing up in their nesting box, and had made them six feet long, four and a half feet high and four feet wide. These dimensions had been carefully worked out to allow the woodpeckers enough room to fly about without enabling them to get too far away from us. The front of each aviary was quarter inch plate glass which would stand up to very rough treatment, while the rest of the aviary was made of strong wire mesh. We had selected a mesh which was free from snags so that the woodpeckers would not damage their feathers, particularly their tail feathers, when they climbed about on it.

We had built the aviary by the side of a pond in a quiet part of the Institute grounds. As there was plenty of sunlight there in the mornings, we would be able to film the woodpeckers when they are most active. To eliminate reflections from the glass we put a black paper shade above and to the front of it. We made a wire frame which could be pushed through an adjustable opening in one side of the aviary to divide it into two. This would prevent the nimble woodpeckers from escaping when we went into the aviary to change the arrangement of branches and tree stumps we had put there.

The aviary's first resident was the great spotted woodpecker which we had had to nurse particularly carefully when it was very young. We took care to ensure that the bird was fully fledged before taking him out of the box, because releasing him in the aviary could have nullified everything that had gone before. If we had transferred the youngster before he was fully fledged, the transition would have been too abrupt. The surroundings would have been strange and fraught with danger, and he would have ceased to recognise us, and become shy and timid. This had to be avoided, so we used to put the box inside the aviary with the youngster in it, before he could fly, leaving the front of the box (to him, his hole) open far enough for him to look out and inspect what were soon to be his new living quarters.

For the first few days we fed him in the box, but later we perched him on a branch and he gradually learnt to know all the tree stumps and branches in the aviary. By the time he could fly he used to leave the box quite readily to be fed and felt at home in his surroundings.

We had reared several youngsters of each of the three species we were interested in—the great spotted woodpecker, the green woodpecker and the black woodpecker—because there was always the chance that one or two might die before reaching maturity. It was also better to have some birds in reserve, because there are individual differences among wood-peckers just as there are among human beings, and we would be able to choose the most suitable for our purposes.

One of the three spotted woodpeckers we had reared was now set free because he was more turbulent than the other two, and would have been a disruptive element in the aviary. We did not put the other two into the aviary together because this would have led to squabbling and fights. We put one into the aviary, and the other one into an auxiliary cage which was only a third of the size of the aviary but adequate for its purpose. We only kept the third great spotted woodpecker in case there were any

116

mishap with the others. Just how easily something could go wrong we were to learn two weeks later.

Up to then we had shot very little film, preferring to wait until the birds' beaks and tail feathers were fully grown, which in the case of woodpeckers is some weeks after they have left the nest.

Once in the aviary, our great spotted woodpecker immediately proceeded to put into practice the exercises with his beak that he had already tried out in his nesting box. Not only did he hammer away at tree trunks and branches, but tried out his beak on the wooden framework of the aviary. We had seen him teaching himself to do this in the nesting box and knew that before long we would have to cover the frame work with strips of sheet iron. But before we had found time to instal these strips, which are essential if one wanted to keep woodpeckers, our great spotted woodpecker had hammered himself out into freedom. When one morning I came to the aviary imitating as usual the bird's call, a woodpecker answered me from the branches of a tall tree. At first I thought it was a strange woodpecker flirting with ours, but then I saw what had happened. I tried every trick I knew to lure him back, but without success. He remained nearby for about half an hour and even fluttered down several times in my direction when I held out some mealworms, but did not dare to come closer than a yard. Then he flew away and disappeared among the oak trees.

For the rest of that day we all tried our hardest to coax him back, but although we saw him at various places and he answered our calls, he would not come close enough for me to feed him and catch him. In the afternoon we tried a new stratagem. We opened the aviary and baited it with a bowl of mealworms, putting some more in a prominent position a few yards away, hoping that this would at least tempt the woodpecker to stay in the neighbourhood of the aviary until nightfall when he might go inside. We waited in vain. Darkness fell, but there was no sign of him. I had to admit that George was right when he said: 'That bird would be foolish to come back to a cage when he can find food anywhere in the forest'. The

117

next morning, after a depressing drive down to the Institute, we thought we were seeing things. There was our woodpecker sitting cheerfully in the aviary and calling loudly for his breakfast. We joyfully fed him all the mealworms he could eat.

A few minutes later we solved the riddle of the woodpecker's return. He had spent the night in the forest and awoken with a hearty appetite. His food bowl was not there, of course, nor was his ration of mealworms. He would certainly have been able to find enough food for himself, but had not yet adapted himself to his new conditions. When one of the assistants at the Institute passed by on her way to work, he had obviously taken her for my wife, who had fed him for so long, and flew over to a tree nearby calling for food. The assistant had heard about our missing woodpecker so she held out her hand invitingly and he flew up to her. She caught him firmly but gently and put him back in the aviary.

The young green woodpeckers got on so well together in the nesting box that we decided to take the risk of putting them together into one aviary. There was more than a slight chance that when we did, they would forget our short acquaintance and revert to their notoriously turbulent, anti-social ways. We need not have worried. The nesting box had been transferred to the aviary a few days earlier, and when we opened the front to feed the woodpeckers they flew up to a nearby branch and immediately reached out their beaks to the food-bowl from which we always fed them with a pair of tweezers.

When woodpeckers have left the nest, they still call to their parents for food, and these youngsters did the same. They inclined their heads slightly and jerked their wings up and down, drawing attention to themselves. When we had fed them they flew off on an inspection tour of their domain, taking no notice of our presence. But their behaviour was quite different from that of the great spotted woodpeckers and black woodpeckers. In their search for food those typical tree-dwellers had immediately set to work with their beaks on the branches and tree stumps of the aviary. The green woodpeckers, however, used their beaks far less and did not hammer so strongly, usually restricting themselves to particularly rotten wood. They threw the bits of bark aside and stabbed into cracks and holes in the wood, using their beaks far less as chisels than as tweezers—though more often they used their tongues instead. These long prehensile organs flashed in and out probing leaves, branches and wire netting—everything that was new to them.

We soon observed that the green woodpeckers were much more interested in the ground than in the trees. However rotten the branches we put in the aviary they still preferred the ground for foraging. They snapped up any insect larvae or pupae they found on a branch, but then immediately flew down to ground level, stabbing tirelessly into compost heaps and piles of cut grass with their probing tongues.

On our expeditions we had often observed green woodpeckers searching for ants' nests in the meadows. Ants form the main part of their diet; and now they were hoping to find an ants' nest in the aviary. Both black and red ants abounded in the meadows near Buldern so we found it easy to keep the green woodpeckers supplied with them. On dry, warm days when the ants brought up their pupae from below ground and carried them into the sunlight, we dug up their nests and took them over to our woodpeckers at the double so that not too many ants escaped. The birds set to as soon as we put the first nest inside the aviary. We had abundant opportunities to observe and film the woodpeckers as they rifled the ants' nests we had brought them. They always hopped towards the centre of the nest which was the favourite depository for the pupae. Then, with quick sideways movements of their beaks they brushed aside the earth in order to expose the pupae.

In their natural conditions when the green woodpeckers come upon an ants' nest in sunny weather they soon find where most of the pupae are and eat enormous quantities of them. But we had dug up and transported the ants' nests to the aviary; the ants had obviously been disturbed and had hidden the pupae in the innermost recesses of the nests. This did not make things quite so easy for the woodpeckers, so first, they cleared

119

away the sun-dried earth on top of the nest, until they reached the passages leading downwards to the pupae. Then their long tongues went into action. We naturally could not observe the movements of their tongues inside the nest, but we did see them dart out of the slightly opened beaks. Each time a woodpecker did this he sank his beak to its full length into the earth and jerked his head back when he retracted his tongue. If his beak and tongue combined were not long enough, then he would dig away the earth using his beak as a spade; these movements resembled those which the woodpecker had used when he brushed aside the earth in order to expose the pupae. The woodpecker does not have much time for this digging because it sends the ants swarming out of the nest. When they go into the attack with their nippers and start squirting their acid the woodpeckers soon give up.

There were many lively scenes when we were filming the woodpeckers gobbling up ant pupae. By ruffling their feathers and making scratching movements with their feet, the woodpeckers would try to keep the ants from crawling up their legs and invading their plumage for long enough to flash their tongues a few times more into the pupal chambers. These efforts usually came to a sudden end when the ants squirted their stinging acid into the woodpeckers' eyes, for even the woodpecker's cornea is not immune against an attack of that kind. The woodpeckers would hop out of range, shake their feathers to clear them of intruding ants and then, standing outside the circle of ants peacefully eat them from the periphery.

Green woodpeckers are very partial to red forest ants and wood ants which make their nests in rotten logs. When we provided a wood ants' nest for the woodpeckers, to film the way they laid bare the pupal chambers with their beaks, we observed that their movements were the same as when they were digging in ants' nests in the ground. This 'ground' woodpecker probes and stabs with great perseverance into soft, decaying wood; but, in contrast to other 'hacking' woodpeckers, as soon as he meets wood that is still firm and hard he gives up instead of using his beak as a hammer or chisel.

120

We had carried out so many observations with other species of woodpeckers that, comparing them all, I thought I could now see in the green woodpecker's use of his beak the original faculties from which the other species had developed their various characteristics. Hazardous though such conjecture may be, I felt I could nevertheless assume that the sequence of events was as follows. Originally woodpeckers used their beaks for digging out food only, just as most small birds still do now. From just probing with their beaks, the woodpeckers then took to pecking away bits of wood; and as their beaks grew stronger they evolved into chiselling tools, so that the birds could the more easily gain access to their prey. Next, the woodpecker learned to hammer its way into rotten wood. Having found that a tree trunk afforded him shelter overnight, he then learned to hollow out a hole in it for himself. Finally, he realised that a hole in a tree trunk was the safest place to rear a brood; and when he could not find one ready-made he hollowed out his own. His constant hammering against branches and trees taught him that when hammering against dry wood he could make signals to attract others of his species. So his drumming became a mating call. Parallel with these developments, his feet and tail evolved their present form. Finally, each species developed its own specialised attributes—the hollowing out of an anvil in which to pulverise food by the great spotted woodpecker, the relief signals of the black wood-pecker, and the use of tongue and beak to hunt for food on the ground by the green woodpecker, which has narrower feet and weaker claws than the other species. All this is of course only conjecture; but the way the young woodpeckers develop in their nests seems to support it, and give it a certain degree of probability.

As soon as we put an ants' nest in the aviary our three woodpeckers hurled themselves upon it, and these were the only occasions when the otherwise peaceable birds squabbled amongst themselves and used their beaks on one another. First they pointed their beaks threateningly, like lances, at their 'fellow guests'. If this gesture had no effect they began to stab at the air in the direction of their rivals. At the same time they jerked their heads from side to side—just as we had seen them do at mating time in spring, when male and female showed their distinguishing markings to each other. The final phase began when the woodpeckers hopped towards each other and gave battle with their beaks. When one emerged victorious the other two would follow to the ants' nest in orderly fashion. Only once did I see two birds use their claws on each other to decide which should have first turn at an ants' nest.

We maintained our contact with the woodpeckers, although we could not always prevent their being frightened when cats and dogs approached the aviary, or when we changed the branches and tree trunks we had put there. When they did get a fright they took refuge in the three nesting boxes we had fixed as overnight quarters to one side of the aviary.

TEN

The Woodpeckers' Anvils

In the nesting box we had made for the great spotted woodpeckers they could do everything that young woodpeckers should do as they grow up: climb about, hammer with their beaks, practice with their tongues. On their first tour of inspection of the aviary they had immediately begun to search for food in typical woodpecker fashion. They did not have to acquire this skill, it was innate. All they needed to do was perfect it.

As soon as our great spotted woodpecker left the 'nest' we noticed that when he was climbing up he constantly tapped his beak against the tree trunk or branch. This seemed to serve two purposes. First, the tapping of his beak disturbed insects hidden under the bark, mossy growths and rotten patches, and as they scurried from their hiding places it was easy for him to snap them up. Second, he seemed to be able to tell from the sound of his beak against the wood whether the particular place he was tapping was worth investigating further. If it was, he would go over to hammering immediately, chipping away small pieces of bark or making a wedge-shaped incision in the tree. Between bursts of hammering, the woodpecker's tongue would flash like lightning in and out of cracks and crannies in the wood. We quite often saw him come upon a beetle larva gallery bored deep into a branch. He had to hack away for quite a time before his tongue could stab in to reach the food concealed there.

To find out whether the great spotted woodpecker could really decide whether there were insects present by tapping on the branch with his beak, we made an experiment. We drilled holes at various places along an oak branch, baited them with mealworms and then closed them up again. The woodpecker was in the habit of thoroughly inspecting every branch or tree trunk we put inside the aviary; so perhaps it was not surprising that he found the first hole we had made and soon had located the other seven. What was astonishing was the speed and thoroughness with which he accomplished this task. I am convinced that this is the way in which the great spotted woodpeckers find most of the larvae that they feed on in the forest.

Our great spotted woodpecker found his work particularly rewarding when we brought him some fir logs thickly infested with bark-beetles. We had acquired them from our friend Hummel, because we had noticed on our expeditions in the forest that the woodpeckers had pecked away all the bark round the feeding places of the larvae. When a particularly heavily infested tree was felled, Hummel said: 'You see what you've done by taking away my woodpeckers for experiments! They are my best pest exterminators!'

We had no sooner put the log inside the aviary than our great spotted woodpecker got to work. A few strokes of his beak were enough for him to work out the best technique for getting at the bark-beetles. Holding his head sideways he hacked at the bark, peeling it away in long shavings like wood under a jack plane. Sometimes he would tear away pieces of bark as big as a man's hand, using his beak as a pair of pincers. He would then fall upon the bark-beetles, their pupae and larvae, gobbling them up at lightning speed.

It was in August, when the hazel nuts ripened, that we made our most interesting observations of the woodpeckers' use of their beaks for foraging. It was then that we gained an excellent opportunity of watching woodpeckers at work at their 'smithies'. Great spotted woodpeckers are very fond of hazel nuts, and to split them open they select certain places on branches and tree trunks and use them as anvils, cracking the nuts

124

against them and removing the kernels. Of course, the woodpeckers rarely find a crack or split wide enough to hold the nut, so they usually have to chisel out some of the surrounding wood.

To get our films, we put some hazel nuts on the ground in the aviary, the first our great spotted woodpecker had ever seen. From the enthusiasm with which he pounced on them it seemed as if he knew that the hard shell enclosed something he liked. Like all 'tree' woodpeckers he did not like alighting on the ground. In the forest great spotted wood-peckers will always land on a log if they can, and hop to the ground from there. This is exactly what our woodpecker did, and he hurried over to the nuts to give them a close inspection. He then pushed hard at a nut with his beak several times until he found that all he was doing was rolling the nut over and over. He did this seven times before realising its point-lessness, and then picked up the hazel nut in his beak and climbed up a nearby tree trunk. He started searching for a suitable place to hold the nut while he cracked it open, and chose a horizontal oak branch. He pushed the nut into a wide crack in the bark and rammed it down as far as he could. He thought that it was securely held and hammered at it with his beak; but it rolled out of the crack and fell to the ground.

This happened several times, and then our woodpecker chose a steeply-inclined branch with a number of small holes in it, which seemed to offer a better chance of success. Again he tapped the nut to ram it home. After the first few strokes of his beak the nut rolled out of the hole, but this time did not reach the ground. The bird was below it on the branch; and as it rolled towards him he whipped his wings forward in a flash and caught it between them. At the same time he pushed his body forward and ruffled his breast feathers to hold the nut more securely.

After transferring the nut to his beak he tried several other places on different branches, but was no more successful than before. Then he seemed to get an idea. Holding the nut in his feathers he set about im-proving his anvil, carving away the wood with his beak. He had to make several attempts before the nut was held fast, but then three blows of his beak were enough to split the shell and lay bare the kernel. He had successfully cracked his first nut.

The next thing we wanted to observe was a woodpecker picking a nut from a tree and fixing it in position on a tree limb at the side of the aviary. It would have been quite easy for a lesser spotted woodpecker to run right along the very thinnest branches, but it was a different proposition for our great spotted woodpecker who was much bigger and heavier. It looked as if he would not be able to pick any ripe nuts at all, because he needed branches which his claws could grip and which would support his tail. He managed to get one nut, however, which he plucked by climbing a strong branch near it.

I assume that the great spotted woodpecker mainly picks up hazel nuts from the ground—as he picks the fir and pine cones which form the major part of his diet for much of the year. During our year with the woodpeckers there were unfortunately no new cones, and the few that we managed to scrape together for our experiments involved a great deal of searching all through the forest. We wanted to find out how the great spotted woodpecker would react when confronted for the first time with a fir cone. Just as he had done with the hazel nut he got to work without hesitation. He seized the cone at its centre of gravity and climbed up to his hazel-nut smithy, but this was too small, so he found a more suitable branch and chiselled out a new anvil.

The woodpecker did not derive much satisfaction from his fir cone, as all the cones we had managed to find were from the previous year; their scales had opened and most of them were empty. However, we did get the chance to see how he dealt with it. First he set the cone upright and then broke off the scales one after the other, picking out the sparse seeds with beak and tongue. Every time the cone slipped out of the hole he had made for it, he improved the shape of the hole, then retrieved the cone and put it back. Fir and pine cones do not differ from each other very much in size (unlike hazel nuts), so the woodpecker did not have to prepare so many anvils. He always sought out steeply inclined branches and trunks because they afforded better purchase for his claws and tail, and he could bring his beak to bear more powerfully, as well as hold the slippery cone or nut fast while he was working. Our woodpecker had been quick to realise what the fir cone was, and he was just as quick to realise the pointlessness of his endeavours. Snapping off the scales from the top called for a great deal of effort, but he found so few seeds that it was not worth continuing, and he quickly lost interest.

Pynnönen made exhaustive observations to find out what woodpeckers live on throughout the year, and these showed that the great spotted woodpecker in Finland lives almost exclusively on pine and fir cone seeds. Only at the end of April or beginning of May, when the cones have opened in the sun and the seeds fallen to the ground, does this woodpecker change over to the larvae and pupae of ants, beetles, spiders and butterflies. During his observations of woodpecker smithies Pynnönen discovered that a great spotted woodpecker dealt with a hundred and thirty-seven pine cones in the course of an eleven-hour day. That makes an average of twelve cones an hour, and since each cone holds about fourteen seeds, the woodpecker's haul was almost nine hundred in a day.

ELEVEN

The Woodpeckers Show Us Their Tongues

Two things about woodpeckers set them apart from the rest of the bird world—their beaks and tongues, and the special ways in which they use them. We had already recorded the virtuosity with which they used their beaks for drumming, tunnelling, looking for food and working anvils. Now we wanted to investigate the way they used their tongues, surely one of the strangest and most remarkable examples of the adaptability of these birds.

The tongue of most birds is short, broad and fleshy and lies in the bottom of the beak. That of the woodpecker is used to catch its food. It is prehensile and several times as long as the beak. The green woodpecker, for instance, can stretch its tongue out four inches beyond the tip of its beak. It is enabled to do this by the highly developed longitudinal muscles connected to the elongated horns of the hyoid bone. They do not end, as in other birds, at the back of the head, but curve upwards to the cranium and then forward (wedged in a broad, deep groove) until they end in front of the eyes. In the green woodpecker the horns of the hyoid apparatus stretch in a broad curve round both sides of the neck and are five times as long as the beak. In the great spotted and black woodpeckers, which stick their tongues inside crevices and cracks in trees, the end of the tongue is like a hardened stiletto with a great number of small barbs at its horny tip. This harpoon-like tongue is particularly suited to the favourite feeding

128

A true wood-borer, the black woodpecker easily opened the pupal chambers and searched every corner of them with beak and tongue

The tongue of the great spotted woodpecker is used like a harpoon. Its hard tip spears the beetle larva, which is then held fast on tiny barbs and withdrawn through the gallery

As we watched our adopted woodpeckers fly off through the trees
our sadness at parting with them was mixed with gratitude

methods of these two species—spearing insect larvae and pupae inside their chambers. They stab into cracks and holes in the wood, impale their victims and draw them out of their sleeping quarters. Their tongues are two and a half to three times the length of their beaks, but this is enough for their purpose, because they can chisel their way into the insect galleries with their powerful beaks.

The green woodpecker does not use his beak so readily, and is moreover a specialist in the art of robbing ants' nests which have galleries running deep into the ground. In addition to its extreme length the tongue of this species has several other remarkable properties. It is flatter and wider at the tip and has no barbs. The saliva glands in the lower mandible are much more strongly developed, and coat the tongue with a slimy secretion to which the bird's hapless victims adhere when it darts its tongue into their chambers.

From our earlier observations we knew how the woodpeckers used their tongues when foraging, but we now wanted to record this on film. It was in fact the objective which had attracted us the most. We could be certain that our protegés in the aviary would use their tongues in the same way as their fellows in the forest. But we had to create conditions in which the green woodpeckers used their tongues directly in front of the camera and in surroundings suitable both for scientific documentation and for ordinary nature films.

During our constant searches for live food for the woodpeckers, we discovered a birch tree which was thickly infested with bark-beetle larvae—although the wood of this tree was so firm that we were able to cut away a segment of the surface and leave most of the galleries and larval chambers exposed. Our plan was to saw off part of the birch trunk and place it on one of the tree limbs behind the glass front of the aviary, with the galleries and larval chambers flat against the glass. Then we should be able to film the woodpecker at work with his tongue.

When we had put the birch log into position, the woodpecker flew up and immediately inserted his tongue in one of the holes, stabbing jerkily

129

in search of the larvae concealed there. But he could not reach far enough since the gallery leading to the larval chamber was two inches long. As he had not yet learned that where there are galleries there is definitely food, he gave up after hacking perfunctorily at the hole a few times. We now knew that the great spotted woodpecker could not reach two inches with his tongue, so we shortened the gallery by a quarter of an inch; and this time he succeeded in reaching his prey. The harpoon point of his tongue stabbed at the curled-up larva until it had pierced through its skin and then began dragging the victim, impaled on the barbs, through the gallery to the exit. Our woodpecker then met with a snag. The gallery narrowed towards its entrance and the larva was too big to pass through it and fell back into its chamber. The woodpecker had to bring his chisel beak to bear and widen the gallery before he could retrieve the larva.

In the course of our observations we discovered that, whether he was investigating a chamber to see if it contained a larva, or whether he was actually impaling one before extracting it, the great spotted woodpecker flicked his tongue in and out of the beetle galleries with the same quick, light movements. This was obviously due less to the fact that the tongue muscles are unable to sustain a prolonged effort than to the even more important fact that the woodpecker must withdraw his tongue in order to give it a fresh coating of its special secretion. This is not necessary for impaling larvae; but with both the great spotted woodpecker and the other species, this rythmical darting of the tongue is inborn, especially because, as the tongue shoots in and out of splits and cracks in the wood, it may also trap many insects which can only be caught by the sticky secretion.

After the great spotted woodpecker had methodically investigated all the galleries in the birch stump and shown us how he used his tongue there were no more difficulties about filming this interesting activity. But there were still some preparations to be made. We could not film in ordinary sunlight, because the shadows thrown by the galleries would be too hard. Without sunlight the galleries would be too dark. We would have to work with a spotlight. Furthermore the woodpecker's tongue flashes in and out so quickly, that an ordinary camera would be too slow to record it. We therefore replaced our handy 'Arriflex' with an 'Askania' which takes eighty frames a second. As film is usually exposed at the rate of twenty-four frames a second, the 'Askania' would give us three times as many pictures of the nimble woodpecker. We wanted the bird's tongue to show up as large as possible on the screen and that meant using the slow-motion camera at very close range, only four inches to be exact. Here a new problem arose, because the camera made so much noise that it was impossible to muffle it enough at such close quarters. It was not surprising that the moment we started filming, the woodpecker withdrew his tongue and either flew off or did nothing at all, so that many precious feet of film were lost.

We husbanded our precious bark-beetles which are usually difficult to come by, and took steps first of all to get the woodpecker used to the whine of the slow-motion camera mechanism. We baited the insect galleries with mealworms and then ran some old film through the camera. After some days the woodpecker had grown so accustomed to the high-pitched hum of the camera that he completely disregarded both it and the spotlight and continued with his foraging. We loaded the camera with fresh film and soon we had recorded examples of all the uses to which this woodpecker puts his tongue.

To film the black woodpecker's tongue we had to employ different tactics. These big birds live on ants, beetles, their larvae and pupae, and other insects such as butterfly pupae, as well as spiders. Black woodpeckers prefer most of all to forage in tree trunks where there are wood ants' nests and other insects. We always tried to create as near natural conditions as possible for each species, so we sawed up some pine logs and put them in the aviary. After cutting away the sides to expose the ant galleries and chambers we arranged the tree stumps so that they faced the glass front of the aviary. The woodpecker could only reach its food with its tongue from above or behind the tree stumps, so that it would be in view of the camera the whole time.

The black woodpeckers were two months old when we first started recording how they used their tongues. During the previous month we had observed their normal activities in the aviary very closely and had noticed that they used their powerful chisel beaks much more effectively when foraging, than their smaller relative the great spotted woodpecker. In the course of a single week they had reduced a healthy twelve-inch oak to a thin stump with their hammering. Throughout the day they hammered away furiously, so it was as well that we had already sheathed the wooden frame of the aviary with wire and sheet iron.

All our woodpeckers were very well fed. There were always reserves of food in the food bowls and we managed to supply plenty of live ants and ant pupae almost every day. The black woodpeckers' furious hammering did not mean that they were hungry, but that they felt an inner compulsion to hammer. They now made straight for the tree stumps we had put in the aviary, because they had seen ants running about on them, and every hammer blow of their beaks made fresh inroads on the swarming insects. As soon as they had opened a new corridor into the ants' nest their tongues flashed into it, but their reach was less than we had expected. We wished to settle once for all just how far their tongues could reach, so we provided them with tree stumps where the pupae lay three and a half inches below the surface. The woodpeckers' tongues should have been able to reach three times the length of their beaks, but we never saw them extended more than two inches. Once the woodpeckers had eaten all the food within range of their tongues, they brought their beaks into action to widen the galleries before again inserting their tongues. Since black woodpeckers are particularly adept at using their beaks, they do not need a specially long tongue.

All that now remained was to film the green woodpecker searching for food with his tongue. Just as we had done with the others, we put tree stumps containing wood ants' nests against the glass of the aviary. It was an astonishing experience to see the green woodpecker shooting his long, sticky tongue into the pupal chamber. It wriggled like a worm through

132

the galleries drawing everything it touched, ants or pupae, relentlessly into the bird's gullet. This long tongue is so liberally coated with sticky saliva by the glands in the lower maxilla that streaks of it are often left on the trees. The way in which it followed every bend and curve of the ant galleries was nothing short of amazing. The woodpecker could push it outwards, upwards and downwards and even curve it back on itself towards his beak. The most mobile part of all is the extreme tip of the tongue, which (in the case of the green woodpecker) has developed into a wide, flat sort of lip. This can be moved about independently of the rest. From close up we could see that the lip is used to feel the location of the birds' food, particularly ant pupae. The lip then becomes a little spoon and scoops the prey out of its chamber to be picked up by the sticky tongue.

We had already spent several days accustoming the green wood-peckers to the spotlights and the whine of the slow-motion camera, but when we wanted to start filming we came up against a snag. Among our four green woodpeckers there was one who was more timid than the rest and did not like us near him. Whenever we brought food to the aviary, three of the birds would fly up to us, while the fourth disappeared inside his hole as soon as he saw us. When we had gone away he came out again to claim his share of the food in the food bowl. We could therefore use only three woodpeckers for filming and were considering releasing the fourth.

If we had done so we should never have been able to shoot what turned out to be one of our most worthwhile scenes. As the result of a chain of unfortunate circumstances, all three tame woodpeckers escaped one afternoon. We had always taken special precautions with them and had put up a small auxiliary structure in front of the aviary entrance. It was like a narrow porch with a second door in it, covered with wire netting and was intended to prevent birds from escaping when we left the door open while carrying branches and tree stumps into the aviary. Un-fortunately, the woodpeckers had tunnelled a way into the porch through the soft earth of the aviary. We had not foreseen anything like this and so

133

had left the door unbolted. Once inside the narrow porch the birds had flown from one end to the other until the continual bumping of their bodies finally opened the door and they flew off.

The timid one had not been able to bring himself to follow his three companions to freedom, so there was still a chance that we might be able to shoot our films. It was a slim chance, however—because shooting slow motion films, even of tame woodpeckers, at four inches' range while using a spotlight is extremely difficult. The only way we could hope to film our remaining green woodpecker was by employing a ruse. He was already used to the cut logs behind the glass front of the aviary, and often searched for food there. What we did was to build a closed, light-tight hide in front of the aviary. We fixed the shiny lid of a shoe polish tin to the side facing the glass, so that the woodpecker would get used to the unblinking eye of the camera staring at him. Then we began to turn up the spotlight very slowly to illuminate the ant galleries, and finally started the camera to get our shy woodpecker used to its sound. He was very suspicious indeed, and for a long time I thought that we had failed. In the end, however, we succeeded in filming him using his tongue. As in most work with animals, patience is essential for success, and the more difficult the task, the more rewarding its successful completion.

In October our time with the woodpeckers came to an end. We should have liked to keep at least the black woodpeckers, and find out whether they would breed in the aviary the following spring, which would have enabled us to film more of their life cycle. But we had to make some biology films and would not have been able to devote all our time to the woodpeckers. We took our adopted woodpeckers back to their native forest where they would best be able to preserve their newly-gained freedom.

When I saw them fly off through the trees my sadness at our parting was mixed with the special satisfaction that our year with the woodpeckers had fulfilled more than our expectations.

Today well over a thousand copies of our film on the life of wood-

134

peckers have been distributed all over Europe. They help to deepen our interest in nature and our understanding of her creatures. This is also the purpose of my book.

The Woodpeckers of Germany and Britain

FIELD MARKS	WEIGHT AND SIZE	VOICE	AREA WHERE FOUND

Green Woodpecker (*Picus viridis*)

Dark green upper parts, pale grey-green under parts, crimson crown, dark moustachial stripe, yellow rump.	$6\frac{1}{2}$–$7\frac{1}{2}$ oz. Size of jay.	A very loud ringing 'laugh'.	Throughout Germany from the plain to more than 5,200 feet above sea level. Prefers deciduous woods, parks and farmlands. In Britain in well-timbered country, from woodlands, commons and farmlands to parks and gardens, preferring deciduous trees.

Grey-headed Woodpecker (*Picus canus*)

Plumage greyer than that of green woodpecker. Male has bright crimson forehead. Female lacks red.	About $4\frac{1}{4}$ oz. Smaller than the green woodpecker.	Call notes resemble those of green woodpecker but becoming progressively deeper and slower.	Mountainous areas and hill country of South, West and Central Germany. Habitat as green woodpecker in Great Britain, but inhabits mountain forests up to the limit of the tree line.

Great Spotted Woodpecker (*Dendrocopus major*)

Black back, large white 'shoulder' patches, crimson under tail-coverts. Male has crimson nape-patch. Young have entire crown crimson.	$2\frac{3}{4}$–$3\frac{1}{4}$ oz. Size of a thrush.	Loud, shrill 'kik' or 'tchik'.	Throughout Germany in forests and parkland. In Britain as green woodpecker but shows more preference for woodlands; prefers conifers in northern England and Scotland.

136

FIELD MARKS	WEIGHT AND SIZE	VOICE	AREA WHERE FOUND

*White-backed Woodpecker (*Dendrocopus leucotos*)

White rump, black back and 'shoulders'. Scarlet crown extending to nape. Female has black crown.	Somewhat larger than the great spotted woodpecker	Like the great spotted woodpecker's or a deeper 'kik' and sometimes two-syllabled 'ki-ik'.	In alpine areas, Bohemian forests and forests and Bavarian forests.

Lesser Spotted Woodpecker (*Dendrocopus minor*)

Very small. Great deal of white on back. Male has dull crimson crown. No red on underparts.	$\frac{3}{4}$–1 oz. Size of a sparrow.	High, repeated 'kee-kee-kee'.	Prefers gardens, parks and mixed forests throughout Germany. In Britain as green woodpecker.

*Middle Spotted Woodpecker (*Dendrocopus medius*)

Resembles great spotted woodpecker, whiter underparts merging into rose-pink. Male, female and juveniles have crimson crown.	2–2½ oz. Size of a starling.	Lower in pitch than that of great spotted woodpecker. 'Ptik-teuk-teuk-teuk-teuk'.	Deciduous forests and parklands with old oak trees.

*Three-toed Woodpecker (*Picoides tridctylus*)

Male has yellow forehead, female with grey forehead. No red. Plumage gives impression of being dark.	About 2¼ oz. Size of a thrush.	Short 'Kek-ek-ek-ek'.	Bavarian Alps, Bavarian and Bohemian forests. Particularly fond of burnt tracts of forest.

* Not found in Britain

137

FIELD MARKS	WEIGHT AND SIZE	VOICE	AREA WHERE FOUND

†Black Woodpecker (*Dryocopus martius*)

Male with red forehead, female with red patch on back of head. Rest of plumage black.	10–11½ oz. Almost the size of a crow.	Loud, whistling 'kleea', high grating 'krri-krri-krri-krrri-krrri', and 'pee-ack' like a jackdaw.	Throughout Germany, particularly in large tracts of well matured coniferous forest and beech woods with old trees.

† Has been reliably reported in Britain several times, but so far has not been accepted to the official British List.

138

Photographic Contributors

Colour plate facing page 80	Hermann Fischer, Warenholz
Plates facing pages 16 and 97	Ella Grenzemann, Harksheide
Colour plates facing pages 48 and 96, colour photograph on front of jacket	Eric Hosking, London
Top of plates facing pages 17 and 56, plate facing page 129	J. Roedle, Pfrondorf
Top of plates facing pages 32 and 33, bottom of plate facing page 56, bottom of plate on back of plate facing page 105, bottom of plate facing page 105	George Schimanski, Munich
Top of plate on back of plate facing page 32, plate facing page 72	E. Schumacher, Munich
Bottom of plate on back of plate facing page 32, colour plate after page 32	Walter Wissenbach, Herborn
Photograph on flap of jacket	J. Roedle
All other plates by	Heinz Sielmann, with the co-operation of the Institute for Films and Pictures in Science and Education